Classic American heavy trucks

Classic American HEAVY TRUCKS

Niels Jansen

UITGEVERIJ
ELMAR

Published 1998 by Uitgeverij Elmar B.V.
Delftweg 147, 2289 BD Rijswijk, Holland in association
with Bay View Books Ltd, The Redhouse, 25-26
Bridgeland street, Bideford, Devon Ex39 2P2

© Copyright Uitgeverij Elmar B.V. 1998

ISBN 1 901432 08 4

Typesetting and design: A/Z grafisch serviceburo b.v.
Den Haag, Holland

Printed in Italy

CONTENTS

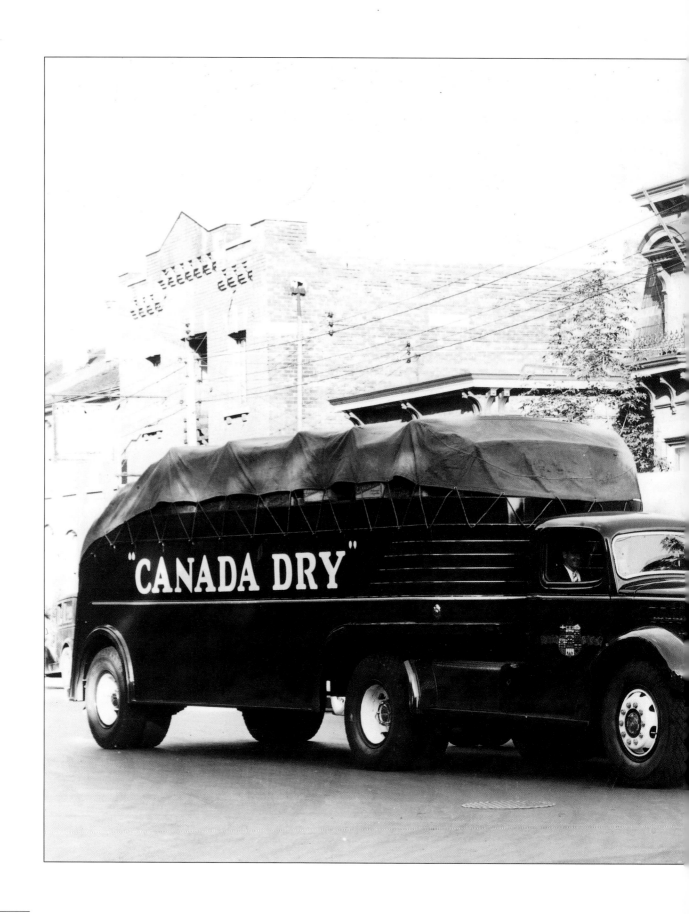

The Mack AC 'Bulldog' could be justifiably called one
of the first true 'classic' truck models. This handsome pair was pictured in New York in 1928.

PREFACE

Since the first commercial vehicles appeared on US roads nearly a century ago, American trucks have fascinated both young and old around the world. No other country has as many trucks as the United States and nowhere else is the cult of the big rig so much woven into daily life. For many decades trucks have been the lifeline of the economy and even today the majority of US communities are dependent solely on motor vehicles.

Through constant development and innovation, the 1998 heavy duty truck has become much cleaner, faster and more efficient than its counterpart of say 30 years ago. Thanks to worldwide liaisons with other manufacturers, American Class 6, 7 and 8 trucks are now much more sophisticated and driver friendly than in the past, yet they retain their unparalleled record for reliability and longevity. On the other hand, take-overs and mergers have caused many well-known names to disappear from the truck market over the last 20 or 30 years. Before World War II hundreds of different truck manufacturers were listed, but now only a dozen or so survive in North America. Admittedly, between them they produce far better products and in much larger quantities than their predecessors ever did, but most of the current models offered by the different companies do not differ much from each other. Just as in the car industry, the demands of aerodynamics and production rationalization have caused virtually all commercial vehicles to lose their individual character. Today, most trucks are lookalikes, often only distinguished by a different badge on the cab or hood. In the past the appearance of heavy trucks did not change as much as passenger cars did from year to year, but at least there were many models that are even today remembered by drivers, operators and enthusiasts with fondness and respect.

In this book we look at a large number of classic heavy duty models that rolled off the assembly lines of all the major, and many of the smaller, American truck manufacturers. In the dictionary 'classic' is described as something 'of the highest quality, or having a value or position recognized and unquestioned'. Another definition is 'traditional'.

To make this volume as interesting and comprehensive as possible a time span of over 50 years is covered. Over 40 American and Canadian manufacturers are represented and their classic models featured.

In some cases it might be questioned whether a particular truck could be called classic or not, but nobody will deny that all the examples presented in this book have contributed in one way or another to the rich heritage of trucking in America, or that they are interesting enough to take a closer look at.

Commercial vehicles, old or new, are more than a viable means of freight transport. Trucks can be beautiful too, and with over 280 high quality pictures, most of which have never been published before, this book hopes to prove just that!

Author's note and acknowledgments

In a century of road transport, many hundreds of more or less successful truck manufacturers came and went in North America. In this book we have tried to give a view of some of the finest classic heavy trucks.

Apart from using picture material from his own archives, the author wishes to thank all the individuals, companies and organizations who kindly submitted information and historic photographs for this book.

In particular, a word of thanks has to go to long-time truck buffs Rolland Jerry, Neil Sherff and Joe Wanchura for their help. Valuable contributions were also made by Larrie Auten, F.H. Bannenberg, Allan H. Berger, Jim Bibb, Wil Davidse, H.C. Demmenie, Nick Georgano, H.R.J. Hoekstra, Ron Knight, P.C. van Mill, Eric Mohr, Martin Phippard, Vern Racek, A.M. and M. van Ramshorst, Arie van Reeuwijk, Larry Scheef, Richard A. Schlicting, Steve St. Schmidt, Bart Vanderveen and Martin Wallast.

Special thanks are offered to the public relations staff of road equipment manufacturers Freightliner, Fruehauf, Heil Co., Kenworth, Oshkosh, Peterbilt and others. We are also indebted to the American Trucking Association, American Truck Historical Society and the Mack Museum.

Last but not least we say thank you to the many writers from the past who have covered the history of trucks and trucking in dozens of reference books and magazines, enabling us to come up with the right facts.

Without the valued assistance of all these people, and others that are not specifically mentioned here, this book would not have been possible.

INTRODUCTION

It was not until well into the 20th century that the favored means of transportation, the horse and cart, was slowly replaced by the motorized wagon. Around the turn of the century few people believed that the primitive, noisy and ugly looking automobile would change the world for good and it was a surprise to many when the motor vehicle soon proved much more reliable, faster and economical than the traditional horse and wagon. Interestingly, in 1901 there were still 17 million horses in the USA! Although the first automobiles could only transport one or two people, motor vehicles soon appeared with a small load space behind, and you could say that these were the first attempts to build a commercial truck. The first production figures for trucks date back to

1904 and amounted to just 411 units; believe it or not, these were produced by no less than 200 different manufacturers! The majority of these 'trucks' were electric wagons, with steam vehicles following close behind.

In 1914 25,375 trucks were produced, while 85,600 units were registered as being operated in total in the USA. By comparison, Canada that same year produced only a meager 384 commercial vehicles. Ten years later the number of commercial vehicles built in North America, including Canada, had risen to a healthy 415,906 vehicles. As said above, many of the early trucks were not much more than converted automobiles with a kind of cargo deck behind, but by 1903 the first 'real' trucks of 2 to 5 ton capacity were

It was not until well into the 20th century that the motor truck finally took over from the horse and wagon.

In 1907 the International Harvester Auto Wagon 'high-wheeler' was praised by farmers who had to bring their wares to market along rutted dirt tracks.

Many early trucks were basically converted automobiles, and Fruehauf figured that pulling a load was easier than carrying one.

being produced by such renowned manufacturers as Diamond-T, Rapid (later GMC), Mack, Reo, Saurer and Studebaker. However, although they may have been called trucks, they did not look much like them and they were certainly not 'classics'. They were merely flatbed wagons with engines mounted up front. The driver sat directly above the engine over the front axle on nothing more than a wooden bench and was totally unprotected from the elements. Cabs and other driver comforts were still unheard of. Yet, despite the primitive nature of the vehicles, the first American motor truck show was held in Chicago in 1907. It was meant to offer the still somewhat reluctant buyers,

many of whom were farmers, a better insight into the benefits of the motor truck over the horse.

In country areas 'high-wheeler' commercial wagons - sort of motorized buggies - were popular for many years. In 1907 International Harvester was the first to introduce these light delivery wagons, which were fitted with huge spoke wheels and had a genuine cargo deck behind the driver. Farmers using dirt roads with deep rutted tracks liked them because of their good 'off road' capabilities. This idea was soon taken up by competitors, among them famous names such as Brockway, Cortland, Riker and Winton.

Other early truck makers skipped the 'high-wheeler' stage and started with the generally much heavier 'engine-under-the-seat' design. Until about 1914 trucks of this configuration predominated in the industry, but just a year later the majority of truck manufacturers switched to a different configuration and installed the engine ahead of the cab, creating the first normal-control truck or 'conventional'.

By this time the external form of most commercial vehicles had taken on a shape that was to see little change over the next 20 years. Even in those early days there was already a marked difference between light duty and heavy duty trucks. The first were mostly based on passenger cars and incorporated many standardized parts. This made manufacturing in quantity easier and also kept the cost of both production and the

vehicle itself down. Heavy trucks, however, were produced mainly in small volumes and they required much more specialized design and manufacturing methods. In the early 1930s this difference became less distinct and even in the lower weight categories the industry was heading towards more specialization. This was done primarily to meet customer demand. At the same time, in an effort to depart more markedly from passenger car design, large volume producers increased the capacity of their trucks from one to one-and-half tons or even more.

In 1912 there was the staggering number of 461 commercial motor manufacturers in the USA, and over the decades this number would rise even further, to well over 2000 in total.

The event that really gave a boost to production and influenced the design and general acceptance of motor trucks was the outbreak of World War I. Between 1914 and 1918, notably in Europe, the demand for simple but reliable heavy duty trucks of American manufacture increased dramatically and as a consequence both Mack and White shipped thousands of trucks to France and England. The war was also responsible for the introduction of the universal USA truck chassis, which was produced by a number of different truck manufacturers. The looks of these USA models may not have been very pleasing, but they proved honest workhorses and performed remarkably well for that time,

even in the most grueling circumstances.

Before the war trucks had only ventured occasionally beyond the boundaries of built-up areas. One reason for this was the lack of decent highways. It was only after World War I that the national highway system slowly took shape. With the help of surplus Army trucks, which were donated to operators in various states by the Federal Government, road transport took a big leap forward in the early 1920s. Ex-Army wagons, particularly with four wheel drive, were put to good use. Equipped with scrapers and tipping bodies

The first motor trucks to appear were of the 'seat-over-engine' type. This is a Sternberg made in Milwaukee.

In the 1910s most commercial vehicles had taken on a shape that was going to see little change over the next 20 years.

Four wheel drive trucks had proved their worth during World War I, and from 1918 they also became invaluable in civilian use.

they proved invaluable in the construction of new roads across the country.

The production of civilian trucks had taken a back seat during the war, but by 1918 truck makers were offering new models again. Manufacturers who built vehicles using solely their own parts were few. They accounted for

only 11 percent of the market, while about 23 percent used various components from other suppliers. The majority of truck builders, however, used as many standardised parts as possible in their assembly. By 1922 there were 242 truck makers listed in the USA.

At this time more handsome models with

The somewhat fragile looking but versatile Ford Model T truck changed the face of road transport in the 1910s and '20s.

closed cabs began to appear on the road. Until then, completely open or very simple box shaped structures were used as cabs. In the 1920s the most popular cab fitted by various truck manufacturers was the so-called C configuration which was used with or without a windshield and at last gave trucks a character of their own. Under the skin the truck was maturing too. The electric or steam powerplant had disappeared in favor of the 4-cylinder gasoline engine which remained popular for a long time because it was of relatively simple construction and it had good lugging ability. Although 6-cylinder gasoline engines had appeared even before 1920 in some truck chassis, it took another ten years of development before they became more common in general heavy-duty trucking. At about the same time, chain drive began to be replaced by bevel, worm and double-reduction rear axles, and the first signs of multi-speed transmissions were there. The change from primitive truck designs and unregulated freight transport to a more reliable and economical trucking industry was a rather slow process, but by 1930 it had finally come of age.

Real classics were few and far between, but if you want to include examples from these early days, the Ford Model T and AC Mack Bulldog are worth a mention. Together, they changed the world of road transport - the fragile looking but handy Ford in the light to medium field, the snub-nosed indestructible Mack in the heavy-duty category.

Also affecting road transport in this period was a flood of new and revised laws. Notably the regulations governing the design and operation of heavy trucks led to a lot of long-term changes in the industry. Until about 1930 the net payload capacity of trucks was hardly more than its tare weight, but from then on models appeared that could easily haul double their own weight, and sometimes even more. Grossly overloaded trucks were the order of the day and most manufacturers built in extra strength. Well-known names like Diamond-T and International even boasted about it. In advertisements abroad these manufacturers said that their products were guaranteed to accept 50 percent excess loading.

Heavier trucks were increasingly used when suitable pneumatic tires became available in the late 1920s. These contributed to vehicles in general becoming much faster and helped make long distance transport a reality. Trucks with solid rubber tires that

had been limited to around town use at maximum speeds of a mere 15 mph could suddenly go up to 45 mph or more once fitted with the new balloon tires. And the vulnerable road system benefited too, because pneumatic-tired heavy trucks caused considerably less damage. The new tires were not designed for ultra-heavy loads though, and at first the problems were numerous. One way to increase payload and to reduce wear and tear on the tires was to fit an extra axle. Hence for many years four-wheel trucks were converted to six-wheelers by outside suppliers. This truck configuration finally became more popular in the 1930s when manufacturers started to offer 6-wheeled models ex-factory too.

These big trucks were constructed not only for the movement of goods in the USA, but also found ready acceptance overseas. The

The so-called 'C' (canopy)-cab, as seen on this early Sterling tanker, remained popular until well into the 1930s.

In the mid-1920s there were still over 240 truck makers listed in the USA! American-LaFrance was one of them.

Seattle, 1929. Kenworth was already a respected name in the West where hauliers required very reliable and sturdy trucks.

Note the very wide cab on this smart looking early 1930s Reo Speed Wagon with Wilson removal van body.

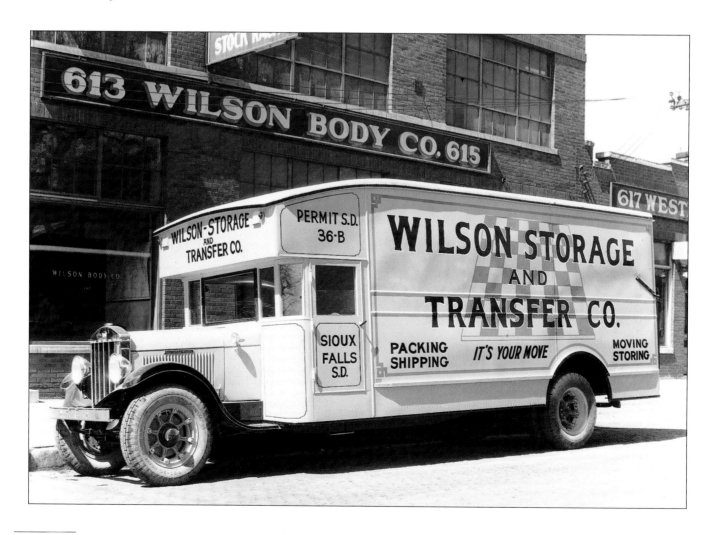

heaviest models had tandem-drive rear axles, a large 6-cylinder gasoline engine, a multi-speed transmission, and air-brakes all round. On 6-wheel chassis the addition of two more air-brakes was very welcome. It was certainly a great improvement on the hydraulically operated brakes that were still used on around 60 percent of four-wheeled trucks in 1930. Electric stop lights came into the picture around this time too, in an effort to prevent rear end collisions when the truck was stopping or slowing down. However, it was 1940 before direction indicators were added as standard equipment on trucks, though in many states their use was not compulsory. What has never disappeared is the American fondness for spoked wheels. Although nowadays made of cast steel, the use of detachable rims dates back to the days of the wooden wheel - but for looks they can not be matched. Striking as have been the changes in the appearance of trucks, notably in the 1930s, most developments were designed for utilitarian rather than aesthetic considerations.

Around 1920 few motor trucks were equipped with proper cabs - a seat, a roof of a sort, and in some cases a windshield, was all the luxury a driver could count on. Side curtains were sometimes fitted for operating in bad weather, but most drivers still had to cope with completely open cabs. The development of fully enclosed cabs that offered more room and comfort for the driver gradually took place during the 1920s and '30s, to the point where truck cabs could almost compare favorably with the comforts of passenger cars of the time. As the 1930s wore on, such luxuries as speedometers, rear view mirrors, sun visors, adjustable padded seats, bulb horns, and vacuum or electric powered windshield wipers were introduced. The latter replaced the hand operated windshield wipers that had first been fitted on trucks in 1920. Of great importance too, was the replacement of old style acetylene gas headlights with much more efficient electric lights. On some trucks the brightness of the headlamps could be controlled by a knob on the dashboard. Improved road

A great example of an early classic truck is this 1932 vintage General Motors Truck (GMC) T90C six-wheeler fitted with a 2400 gallon Heil tank body.

The Mack BX was a powerful and sturdy truck built until 1940, but looking at the size of the driver the small cab was quite outdated by that time!

1930s that more streamlined designs made inroads. Watertight and full length doors with sliding windows added to driving comfort by reducing reflections and glare coming from the side. By around 1935, for most manufacturers, styling had also become a factor in truck design. Crude box shaped structures were discarded in favor of well built all-metal cabs that not only had greater strength and lower weight but were also much more appealing to the eye. The change in appearance of trucks contributed significantly to the modernization of road transport and the acceptance of commercial vehicles by the general public. In the 1930s truck owners also became aware of the advertising potential of their vehicles on the road.

illumination greatly increased safety at night and helped make high speed long distance night operation become a reality. The 1930s even saw dome lights appear in truck cabs. Another contribution to safety and comfort that came along towards the end of the 1930s was the introduction of heaters and defrosters to keep the windshield free from ice and snow. Other milestones that enhanced safety in the 1930s included the adoption of new manufacturing methods in the construction of all-steel cabs which made it possible, among other things, to reduce the width of windshield pillars, thus reducing blind spots.

Sloping windshields to reduce glare at night had been fitted to some trucks as far back as 1929, but it was not until the mid-

For economic reasons annual model changes were usually only made in the light-to medium-duty field. These commercials were mostly turned out by passenger car manufacturers, who could more easily cope with the considerable cost of designing and tooling that is necessary for new models due to much larger production numbers. Hence in these weight categories (and that counts for some truck manufacturers even today) annual changes in appearance have been much more significant than in the heavy-duty sector. There is little reason to come up with a new-look truck each year in the oilfield or logging industry, for example, though of course there has always been a distinction between trucks built for different vocational uses.

In the course of the 1930s trucks began to look more fashionable with hood and fender assemblies that sometimes closely resembled passenger car lines of the day.

The dramatic changes in the design of truck cabs and bodies during the 1930s were made not only for the sake of appearance but also for practical purposes. The strength of cab and fender assemblies was much increased by incorporating more rounded off corners in cowls and cabs, and ease of maintenance was enhanced by the use of front-opening, rear-hinged hoods. The adoption of fancy grilles on the front end of trucks was not just to improve the visual impact, but to protect the radiator core against damage. Even chrome plating was a means of prolonging component life and not just a styling exercise. Quite a few operators, notably in some countries abroad, did not want eye catching chrome parts at all, claiming that certain shippers might be put off by the expensive look of a truck. For these users truck makers like Diamond-T, International Harvester and White produced a series of no-frills export chassis that had all the good qualities but lacked the chrome parts.

There has always been a big difference in the finishing of trucks. Some vehicles looked as if they had left the assembly line before painting, others received a time consuming varnish and enamel finish with a glitter and depth of gloss that resembled the finest furniture of the time. Attention to detail was astounding on some of these early trucks, with striping and gold leaf lettering applied with skill and pride. Although spray painting was offered by commercial vehicle manufacturers as far back as the mid-1920s, many truck owners and coachbuilders hung on to brush methods.

For many years quite a few truck

Although wind resistance was not such a big issue, the quest for more attractive trucks led in 1936 to the design of this intriguing Diamond-T streamline tanker.

In the mid-1930s a move towards 'cab-over-engine' styling came about when the government laid down new length and weight regulations. This sturdy looking White 800-Series armoured van was used to transport valuables.

A view of the assembly line in Building Number 24 of the White Company where production of the classic 700-Series truck is in full swing.

manufacturers had some sort of joint marketing agreement with one or more body builders, and as a consequence a good number of truck chassis offered by different manufacturers had the same basic cab mounted. Volume producers, such as Chrysler, Ford and General Motors, who had considerably more cash to spend and who possessed the pressed-steel techniques to build passenger cars, often designed and built their own cabs for trucks too. Some of these structures also appeared on badge engineered trucks for home and export markets. Apart from the more or less look-alike assembly line products, there were also some very unique cabs. Some body builders managed to come up with streamlined designs that were so advanced that they would not look out of place today. The amount of time and labor that went into these bodies was enormous and they did not come cheap - but you sure got noticed on the road! The unusual shape of many commercial vehicles in the mid-1930s was not only dictated by the general design trends of the period, for dramatic

change in truck development was also led by restrictions that the federal government imposed on road transport from 1933 onwards. To overcome legislative hurdles, truck engineers frantically tried to come up with new ideas. Streamlining was just one of them, while other novelties were the use of lighter materials such as aluminum, the design of drop frames, sleeper cabs, short-coupled semi-trailers, and the (re)intro-duction of the cab-over-engine chassis. The latter would play an important role in trucking for over half a century until in 1982 new federal length laws made this design, at least in the USA, less common.

It is believed that the world's first tilt cab truck was built by the Pope Manufacturing Company in Hartford, Connecticut, in 1912. Although cab-over-engine chassis were built the world over right from the start, the USA became the undisputed leader in the much heralded development of tilt cabs. The greatest benefit of this design was (and still is) the unparalleled access to the engine and other chassis hardware without having to dismantle anything. Cab-over-engine trucks were for many years outsold by the more common designs with a short or long hood up front and the driver sitting behind the front axle. The change in truck styling came about in the mid-1930s when the federal government laid down new length and weight regulations for commercial vehicles. Also city streets became so congested that conventional trucks were almost impossible to maneuver around without causing problems. Cab-over-engine models with their shorter overall length not only solved part of this problem but also could carry more weight on the front axle, thereby improving total weight distribution.

Many of the first COE designs were actually not much more than a chassis of conventional layout on which a flat fronted cab was mounted. As a consequence the driver sat with either all or at least a large portion of the engine in the cab. Not surprisingly, manufacturers had a hard time making the life of the man behind the wheel bearable, as heat insulation and noise suppression techniques were still in their infancy. By the end of the 1930s, however, continuous research into spring suspension, the application of new insulating materials, better seat positions and other techniques had achieved together a much improved COE working environment. The shorter length of the COE was also an advantage when the vehicle was used as a tractor, since compared to a conventional tractor a COE could pull a much longer trailer under the new overall

length restrictions. In 1936 total sales of COE trucks and tractors amounted to around 4500 units, but by 1941 this number had risen to a creditable 32,000!

The adoption of the Motor Carrier Safety Act and the start of the Interstate Commerce Commission activities in 1935 led to great changes in the trucking industry. Transport of freight by road not only increased, but also became much more mature. Interstate trucking particularly got a healthy boost and this in turn led various manufacturers to develop much bigger and better trucks.

Although full- and semi-trailers had been in use since the early 1920s, it was not until the mid-1930s, when more powerful trucks and tractors arrived, that large articulated

This handsomely styled GMC T14 van turned many heads in 1938 on the roads of Great Britain.

A line-up of various great classics from Diamond-T, Chevrolet, International, and Ford in Detroit in 1936.

Pre-war Hendrickson COE tanker doubles still going strong in Chicago around 1947.

different types of 'Streamliners' were built in quantity, all using White/Fruehauf running gear and bodies made by Smith Bros. Another remarkable streamliner of the 1930s was the 'Doodle-Bug' tanker created by the Heil Company on a 1934 Diamond-T rear engined chassis. Several of these radically streamlined 1500 gallon tankers were built for Texaco's airport duties. They incorporated such oddities as double glazed windows and a microphone in the engine compartment so that the driver could hear the rear mounted engine better!

The 1930s also witnessed an increasing use of the sleeper cab, which originated around 1930 when long distance truck operation had become more and more significant. This new development in truck design permitted one driver to operate the vehicle while the other rested or slept. These first sleeper cabs were all integral structures, with the full-length bunk placed transversely behind the driver's seat. Factory-built separate sleeper boxes first appeared in the West just before World War II, designed by Kenworth engineers who had been asked by a line haul driver if it was possible to move his sleeping bunk, which was situated in the head of a van trailer, to a place on the chassis behind the truck cab. Although ride comfort had improved significantly during the 1930s due to the introduction of pneumatic tires and better springs, sleeping in a moving truck was not really a joy until more sophisticated air-suspension systems came in much later. In the 1930s Americans showed the world how

combinations gained ground. Unfortunately, regulations on the overall length for trucks were tightened at about the same time, and that forced manufacturers and operators to look for new ways to maximize payload. Shortening the distance between the front of the trailer and the rear of the truck cab seemed a possibility and closer coupling was achieved by rounding off the front end of the trailer. Apart from gaining more interior load space, this also made the combination more aerodynamic. Although wind resistance was not as a big an issue as it is today, some very intriguing ideas about streamlining trucks saw the light in the 1930s. A classic example is the White 'Streamliner' beer truck that the famous French/Russian engineer Count Alexis de Sakhnoffsky designed for Labatt's in Canada. Between 1936 and 1947 four

When World War II hostilities had finally ended, ex-US Army trucks such as this Mack NR, converted by Steyr in Austria, found ready acceptance in civilian use.

◄ Improved roads and the introduction of reliable diesel trucks such as the mighty Mack LTLSW in 1947 helped make long haul trucking become an important sector of the industry.

Bottling Industry White

VOCATIONAL STUDY NO. 6

useful sleeper cabs could be for long haul trucking, and, partly due to much more liberal overall length limits, US manufacturers have led in their design ever since.

Another development that intrigued many in the early 1930s, and that would have far flung consequences for trucking in years to come, was the diesel engine. As early as the 1920s several manufacturers were experimenting with diesel power in truck chassis, but for practical use its fuel savings did not make up for high initial costs, repair difficulties due to its complicated construction, its rather high weight and, at

► In 1946 there were 65,000 trucks active in the bottling industry, and stylish new Whites played a major part in it.

least in the beginning, its excessive exhaust fume production. Together these were major problems which hampered its progress, but in 1932 Indiana became the first truck manufacturer to offer a model with a Cummins diesel engine ex-factory, soon

▼ In 1949 only 4485 diesel trucks were sold, but a year later the number had climbed to 12,682. This magnificent Cummins powered Autocar Model DCS-100-TN with Utility Vans operated in California.

By 1940 International also offered a choice of diesel engines in its heavy trucks. This long-nosed Model DRD-70 was powered by the popular Cummins HB-600 diesel unit.

In the years preceding the war some great new trucks appeared on the market. Some models that still come to mind today are the beautifully shaped Diamond-T models of the mid-1930s, the Ford V8s, International's C-, D- and K-Line models, 1930s Mack B-series, and E-series conventional and COE models, the massive GMC 90/95 models, the Studebaker 'Big Chief', and White's handsome 700/800-series. Of course there were many more famous models, but these are just a few highlights from this important decade when trucks and road transport finally became mature.

In 1941 there were more than 4.8 million trucks of all shapes and sizes in use in the USA, and 56 percent of them were operated by one-truck owners. Nine out of ten trucks built during World War II were of the conventional type. The 6x6 drive GMC 2.5 ton general cargo truck, of which over half a million were built for worldwide use, is a fine example of a military 'classic' from this era. Over the period 2,600,887 trucks plus 529,647 trailers were produced in America for military service.

Although the design and construction of heavy (off-highway) trucks had made huge advances from a technical point of view during the war years, the changeover to peacetime production did not happen overnight. Shortage of materials was one reason, lack of modern new designs another. Hence most manufacturers pulled out the old model range catalog from before the War and started to offer these products once more to

followed by Sterling and Kenworth. However, old records show that five years later only 2500 diesel trucks were on the road in America.

Towards the end of the 1930s the quality of diesel engines had improved, and due to their high torque rating and good fuel economy they soon became a competitive factor in all sorts of on- and off- highway applications. By the end of the decade the simple 'one truck model' had almost disappeared. The list of optional extras and the variety of specifications that a truck buyer could choose from became almost endless. Around the outbreak of World War II, virtually all manufacturers were able to offer a modern good looking truck or tractor with an extensive range of engine, transmission and rear-axle combinations.

In 1938 Federal introduced an attractive styling with chrome plated grille and round contours that continued through 1950.

prospective buyers. In 1945 the American Trucking Association reported that nearly 200,000 trucks operating in the USA dated back to the 1920s! The ones that had more recent 'birth certificates' consisted mainly of Army surplus vehicles and converted passenger cars. New vehicles were only allocated in very limited numbers to private operators and this was the problem for truck users around the world. On the other hand, this was also the time when the ex-US Army truck became recognized the world over for its unrivaled sturdiness and tenacity in the transportation of civilian goods under the quite challenging postwar road conditions. This undoubtedly also helped new American truck registrations abroad: in 1947 267,379 chassis were exported overseas.

Technically the mid-1940s were not very fruitful. Developments that made headlines did not really occur before the 1950s when labor disputes and shortages of raw materials were over. Soon, every truck manufacturer came up with a completely new line-up. Heavier trucks had proved their worth during the war and diesel powered '18-wheelers' became the standard in long

distance road transportation. To accommodate these bigger trucks many new Interstate highways and private toll-roads were constructed. Diesel power finally took off in this decade. In 1949 only 4485 diesel units were sold; a year later the number had climbed to 12,682, but this still was only 1.3 percent of the total US truck population. In 1950 no less than 1,377,261 trucks were produced in America, but despite the huge number of newly registered vehicles, every third truck on the road in 1953 still dated back to the 1930s!

With the owner-operator market becoming increasingly important, the choice of engines, transmissions, clutches, front and rear axles and suspensions, as well as numerous smaller components, became almost endless. In typical American fashion, buyers could specify exactly what they wanted installed in their trucks. Big trucks became more stylish too in an attempt to change the poor image that the fast growing transport industry had created in the eyes of the average household. Some of the finest truck designs ever created evolved in the 1950s: the B-series Mack, the GMC

Along the lines of the NR military model, Mack came up with the utilitarian looking Model LF and LJ for civilian use in 1940. Pictured is a classic Michigan-doubles headed by a LJT tractor of 1948.

During the 1950s big trucks like this magnificent Diamond-T 950 became more stylish, increasing sales to owner-operators.

A pair of classic Reo and GMC long haul rigs parked up for a break in Joliet, Illinois, in 1957.

'Cannonball', International R-Line, Reo 'Gold Comet', Diamond-T 900 series, White Super Power models, Ford F-series, Sterling J-series — not forgetting the big Kenworth 'Bull Nose', and both Freightliner's and Peterbilt's 'Bubble-Nose' from the West Coast.

Unlike passenger cars, the design of heavy trucks has not changed annually during the last half century. Partly due to increasing costs of development, new models were designed to last at least 10 years before a radical change in appearance and equipment was made. In the 1960s the trend towards larger and more powerful truck combinations

▲ Although driver comfort was much improved after the War, the interior of this White WB still looks quite spartan compared to today's offerings.

continued and radical deviations from the norm were becoming rare. Trucks, and notably cabovers, all started to look the same because they had to comply with new directives sent from above to reduce noise and smoke levels, improve safety, and offer the driver a better working environment. To improve chassis and engine accessibility, tilt cabs became the standard in the 1960s, and to make trucks more durable and manageable there was an increase in the use of

▲ Different operating conditions led to bigger and lighter truck combinations on the West Coast, such as this aluminum-bodied Freightliner Model 800 of 1948.

These brilliant shots taken in Chicago of 1955 and Los Angeles of 1957 represent the heyday of classic trucks.

Specialist manufacturers made huge advances in the design and construction of heavy off-highway trucks during the war years. This 1941 Hendrickson Model A375F looks well up to its task.

lightweight materials such as aluminum, fiberglass and plastic. The latter material in particular led some American manufacturers to design models that were radically different from the standard. A classic example is the 1960s White 5000 cabover with its rounded lines and deep drop windshield. But despite its advantages, the non-rusting plastic cab proved too expensive to produce. Another novel engineering feature that disappeared from the market after many years of testing

was the gas turbine engine. The reason it never made it was the high cost of production and of fuel. Although virtually all heavy truck manufacturers tried to gain ground in the 1960s and 1970s with a gas turbine powered truck, none made it beyond the prototype stage. For heavy trucking nothing could beat the economy and reliability of diesel power. Some West Coast drivers claim, however, that as late as the early 1960s the big Hall-Scott 400 and Buda gasoline and LP gas engines could still outperform in the mountains any diesel unit on the market. In 1969 an amazing 67 percent of all trucks produced were still fitted with eight cylinder gasoline engines! But in the upper weight class diesel power had taken over for good - and so had uniformity in styling. Notably in the 1970s, local and foreign joint agreements and mutual parts sourcing influenced the design and production of heavy trucks more and more. Gone were the days of the uniquely and beautifully styled truck models that had been so typical of individual manufacturers in the past. Because of the enormous costs involved in the development and production of brand new heavy trucks, many famous names died a slow death or were taken over by a more successful, and generally much larger, competitor. Whether these new giants will ever produce a 'classic' today, only time will tell ...

In 1953 diesel fuel was 15 cents per gallon and the big Kenworth 'Bull-Nose' was King of the Road.

The Ford C-750 Big Job six-wheeler with 256 cubic inch Power King V-8 gasoline engine made an impressive sight in 1955.

Although Dart of Kansas City also produced some highway models until 1950, they became best known for their off-highway trucks such as this military-based T13 logging unit.

This classic White WC26 Super Power integral sleeper tractor of 1954 vintage was superbly restored by its Canadian owner.

Some classic trucks just keep on going, like this 1950s Peterbilt Conventional spotted in 1990 somewhere in Indiana.

Two fine 1950s classics still in active service with the Fire Department of White Mountain, California.

Old commercial vehicles are fun and meetings like the annual Antique Truck Show in Macungie, Pennsylvania, bring out the finest in classics.

▼ After the war GMC returned to the styling set in 1939. Navajo Freight Lines ran this incredible 4-71 GM diesel powered ADFR-Series tandem tractor with sleepercab on long distance service in the southwest.

◄ When Sterling took over the Fageol sales outlets just before the war, the make became quite popular in the West. This long wheelbase RWS160H-model with dromedary box was photographed in 1958 on US-99 near Gorman.

In 1953 Freightliner introduced this unusual four wheel drive WF-5844T tractor to pull doubles over tough mountain passes in the Pacific Northwest.

According to some historians, the legendary B-model Mack, first seen in 1953, can be labelled as the finest classic truck ever.

On the West Coast the Peterbilt Model 350 'Bubble-Nose' became a classic. It was produced from 1952 to 1956.

With 47,459 units built the Mack B-61 became the secondbest selling Mack model of all time, finding ready acceptance around the world.

In the 1950s the International DCO/VCO and the Hendrickson COE shared the tilt cabover designed by Diamond-T.

With new directives set by the government, cabovers started to look much the same in the 1960s. Here a Diamond-T 931C and a Ford W-1000 take a welcome break.

One of the most famous cab-share projects evolved in the 1950s when International sold its stylish "Comfo-Vision" cab to almost a dozen smaller truck makers. Apart from the R-190 International, the pictures show a 1956 Diamond-T Model 660, a 1955 Canadian built Leyland Diesel, and a Hendrickson BD-670 dump truck all sporting the same cab.

Another (almost) classic example of different manufacturers teaming up their expertise was seen in the 1960s when the sturdy Mack F-Series sleepercab also appeared on the Brockway 400 and the Hayes Clipper.

Despite rather low production numbers, some of the smaller and specialist manufacturers managed to come up with very pleasing designs, like this aluminum FWD CO-64 from around 1972.

Ford introduced its C-Series low profile cabover in 1957. This popular model was made until 1990 and achieved the longest production run of any vehicle in the company's history.

Brockway is a name remembered with fondness by many. The high cabbed, good looking K359 model appeared in 1965 and was liked for its improved visability and engine access.

Whether a truck is a classic is not just a matter of its age. This colorful beer-hauling GMC 9500 with its extra long hood pictured in Texas in 1970 looks great from every angle.

The Thoroughbreds

When Autocar switched to the manufacturing of motor trucks in 1908 it concentrated on the 'seat-over-engine' model. These first designs did not look pretty but they proved invaluable work-horses.

According to the Motor Vehicle Manufacturers Association, in 1913 23,500 trucks were built in the USA. In total, there were at the time around 300 manufacturers actively producing electric and gasoline vehicles. Right from the beginning there have been two major streams in the truck manufacturing business: first there were the mass producers of passenger cars who also offered commercial vehicles, and second there were the manufacturers who built only trucks. The first group produced mostly a range of light- to medium-duty commercial vehicles that were for the greater part based on their passenger car line. Those that operated independently from the car industry concentrated primarily on the manufacture

of the heavier types of truck, and quite often on the production of buses too. In this field we find the most respected names in American truck history, such as Autocar, Brockway, Diamond-T, Federal, Mack, Reo, Sterling and White. These were all quality manufacturers from the beginning and each designed and built more 'thoroughbreds' in the heavy class than the mass producers together could dream of.

Their success was due to their ability to tailor a truck exactly to the needs of their customers, which the mass-producers of car-derived commercials could not or would not do. To beat the high costs of development and production the latter standardized more and more, while the 'thoroughbreds', on the

The legendary Mack 'Bulldog' was the first production truck that featured a steel roof ex-factory. Note the triple tires and neat 'trailer' sign on this 1929 vintage tanker.

other hand, offered an increasing range of 'trucks made to measure'. These manufacturers asked prospective buyers to come in and specify a truck model that would best suit their hauling needs. Even in the 1920s, the 'real' truck manufacturers recognized that an operator hauling a load of sand or gravel over unpaved roads could not do the job with the same truck design as a man who merely delivered light packages around town.

Although these 'thoroughbreds' were never produced in the huge numbers that the mass producers could achieve with their heavily standardized ranges, their popularity grew steadily through the years. In this field customer satisfaction was high and repeat orders more the rule than the exception. Much better durability figures and higher resale prices were also important factors in making these tailor-made trucks a more popular option for many hauliers.

Before 1930 virtually all American truck producers built vehicles that were assembled for the most part from components which were commonly available on the market. In later years some truck producers, with Mack in front, turned to the manufacture of fully integrated vehicles. Trucks like this were almost completely built from in-house manufactured parts, as European truck manufacturers had been doing for years. Clearly, in the early days the need for individually designed and engineered trucks was less urgent than in the heyday of trucking in North-America just before World War II, and later again in the 1950s and 1960s, when road transport finally came of

age for good. Before and during World War I commercial vehicles were as much standardized as possible. This was partly caused by the government, which had laid down detailed directives for the design and construction of military trucks. In 1917 the US-Army ordered 10,550 general cargo vehicles from six different truck manufacturers. It kept Mack and White, among others, busy for years, building up to 300 standardized army trucks per day each.

During this period Mack designed and produced what is believed to be the world's most famous truck, the AC model. This early

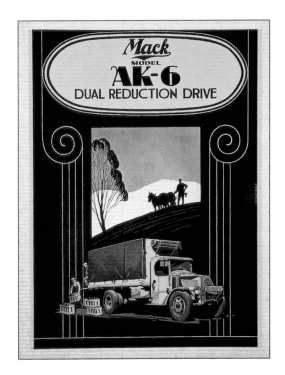

The Model AK was built from 1927 to 1936, but with 2819 units made it lagged way behind the AC's production run of 40,299.

A fine scene of a beautiful late 1920s Sterling EWS27 with trailing axle transfering a load of mineral water from a Chicago and North Western Line boxcar.

A real classic is this stylish Diamond-T six-wheeler with 5-compartment 1500 gallon tanker operated by Texaco in 1932.

heavy-duty truck proved extremely reliable during World War I and because of its tenacious capabilities and its ugly snub-nosed snout the British fighting on the battlefields of France called it the 'Bulldog Mack', as it reminded them of their country's favorite dogs. When the war was over Mack Trucks was quick to see the value of this title and an appropriate hood ornament was designed. Ever since, the Bulldog mascot on the hood and the name have been synonymous with

high quality and Mack.

The AC, with its no-frills look, rugged power plant, simple controls, massive chassis, and heavy-duty chain drive not only changed the course of the War but also helped to make America the Number One industrial nation in the world. Between 1916 and 1938 no less than 40,299 AC models were fabricated. Many of these were used in building highways, cities and dams, hauling logging, mining and oilfield material, and performing a thousand

and one other transport tasks. The Bulldogs introduced in 1915 were built in three capacities, 3.5, 5.5 and 7.5 tons. The first models were powered by a 74hp gasoline engine and had a 3-speed transmission. Other features that set them apart were a pressed steel chassis and a semi-closed steel cab. The AC was in fact the first production truck that had a steel cab complete with roof ex-factory. In the 1920s other snub-nosed Bulldogs appeared on the market, such as the AK, AL and AP models, but neither could match the enormous production run of the famous AC. The AP, for example, the heaviest in the field, was only good for a total of 285 chassis in 12 years. However, equipped with six big spoke wheels and a powerful six-cylinder engine, it sure looked impressive on paper and in the flesh. The AC Bulldog and its relatives can definitely be called one of the first real 'classic' trucks.

In later years Mack would give us several other striking truck models that still live on in the mind, such as the beautifully lined EH and EQ conventional and the popular EF cab-over-engine model, which were introduced between 1936 and 1938. The latter replaced Mack's earlier cab-over-engine design, the 'Traffic' type, which was first introduced in 1934. For its time it was quite a luxury truck with leather-covered spring seats, a well insulated engine, drop-type ventilator windows, an electric ventilator, dome light and even coat hooks. In the following years some of these features found their way to other Mack models. One thing though that most trucks of these days lacked was room in the cab. The 1930s Mack B-series was also fitted with a rather narrow cab that offered very little seat and elbow room. For a small driver it might be sufficient, but a tall man could easily find himself driving in a very cramped position. By 1941 most truck cabs had therefore increased at least 10 inches in width and also had considerably more leg room, better positioned controls, and

The big brute White Model 642 with 6-cylinder gasoline engine made a handsome and sturdy transporter in 1931.

Before World War II, Brockway was among the largest truck makers in America, turning out over 5000 units per year. This Model 150 dates back to the early 1930s.

This Mack BJ tractor pulling two streamlined beer trailers really looked the part in 1932 on the roads of Canada.

improved adjustable seats. Mack was also in the forefront of engine technology, claiming to be the first truck manufacturer to introduce its own diesel engine: in 1938 a six-cylinder diesel of 131hp was offered ex-factory. A year later the famous 'Thermodyne' engine, giving high power and torque through combustion control, saw the light of day. The Bulldog was alive and kicking before the War, selling 5513 trucks and buses in 1937, which was good considering that Mack products sold for rather stiff prices. Today, 1930s Bulldogs are some of the most sought-after models collected and restored by vintage

truck enthusiasts in America.

Towards the end of the 1930s most manufacturers were offering heavy-duty trucks that could be supplied with a whole range of engine, transmission and rear axle combinations and in 1939 total sales of trucks and buses in the USA amounted to 700,377 units. Diamond-T was a make that lives on in the minds of millions of Americans. After producing passenger cars for some years, in 1910 the company's founder Charles A. Tilt was asked by an owner of a Diamond-T motor car to design a

truck. It soon became a success and a few years later the car business was dropped and the company became a full-time truck manufacturer. By 1930 trucks with the diamond shaped logo up front could be seen operating in 60 countries around the world! Diamond-T trucks were not only well built but also incorporated many features that were ahead of their time. Among these were things such as a fully enclosed cab that had rubber suspension, and steel spoke wheels. Although early 1930s' Diamonds did not look bad, in 1936 C.A. Tilt became personally involved in the design of an all-new range of trucks that combined high quality engineering with beautiful styling. Chrome-plating was prominent on these new conventional and cab-over-engine models, and not only the bumper and radiator — the cowl plates, headlights, wheel covers, and running boards also received the shiny treatment. For certain markets abroad Diamond-T offered the same models without all the chrome, because they found that not every owner wanted a truck that looked so 'expensive'!

The 1930s were undoubtedly the most 'classic' years for Diamond. Trucks designed in this period could easily be recognized from a distance and had a styling which was so beautiful that it could only be matched by some of the high quality automobiles of the time. Diamond-T trucks, however, were not built like Mack vehicles. They were purely assembled products using almost entirely

Long before Sterling took over Fageol's sales outlets in 1939, some diesel powered chain-drive models were popular with operators on the West Coast.

By 1932 standards the White 691 Super Heavy Duty Tractor with its wide hood and spacious cab was ahead of its time.

engine sub-frame. Diamond-Ts became notably popular in dispatch services among high profile companies. In 1935 alone over 11,000 units were produced.

Like Diamond-T, White also adapted passenger car styling for its truck models in the mid-1930s. A raked and chromed radiator grille, V-shaped windshield, luxurious steel cab and deeply skirted fender assembly made the advanced 'thoroughbreds' stand out from the many square and boxy designs that were still around. White's handsome new range of streamlined trucks and buses was introduced in 1935. The models that were designed by industrial ace Count Alexis de Saknoffsky were an immediate success. Where White had sold just 1384 trucks and buses in 1933, two years on production reached over 4000 units. After the launch of the good looking 700-series in the mid-1930s, the basic shape of the White conventional did not change much for over 15 years. Even the WB and WC 'Super Power' models of the early 1950s had the same pre-war styling — yet they were beautiful trucks from every angle. And so was the slippery White 3000 COE that was introduced in 1949 when the company cele-brated its Golden Anniversary. With its hydraulically tilting cab, low driving position, wide track and short wheelbase it was an all new concept in trucking and although these features made it an expensive truck, the 3000 sold in considerable numbers. In addition it stimulated a new interest in the tilt cab design. Today it is regarded by many as the

components bought in from third parties. Even the stylish steel cab with V-shaped windshield came from an outside coachbuilder (McLaughlin), and so did the rugged chassis rails (A.O. Smith). Engines were mostly Hercules, albeit modified to Diamond-T specifications, and transmissions and rear axles came from Clark and Eaton respectively. Every truck was built for durability and good looks, as well as ease of maintenance. The COE model of 1937, which was shaped like the famous streamlined train, the Burlington Zephyr, incorporated novel service features such as a slide-out

A real beauty: this 6-cylinder Federal beer wagon must have turn-ed quite a few heads with its sleek lines in 1933.

best example of a 'classic' cab-over-engine truck.

In 1951 the White Motor Company acquired another 'classic' name in the truck field, Sterling. At best, annual sales of this much heralded truck builder never reached more than a few hundred units, but this Wisconsin firm produced some of the most fascinating models ever, such as the rare J-model conventional that was produced from 1937 to 1941. Although it had the basic Sterling steel cab the most striking feature was its long hood with the unusual iron grille-work. Together with the big pontoon fenders and its interesting technical specification, which included chain-drive rear axles and a wood-lined chassis, it made for a very intriguing truck. Only few were built and those mostly went to customers on the West Coast where Sterling had taken over some sales outlets from Fageol after its demise in 1939.

Federal is another 'thoroughbred' that produced some beautiful classic truck models during the 1930s. The early 1930s 'Big Six' was an impressive truck indeed, especially as a six-wheeler, but its boxy styling did not differ much from the competition. A change in design came in 1934 when Federal fitted a slightly slanted one-piece windshield (without sun visor) and a V-type radiator grille. When streamlining became the big issue a year later, Federal announced its good looking '25th Anniversary' model line. From then on to well into the 1950s Federals would sport stylish steel cabs with V-type windshield, high crowned fenders, a long hood with rounded grille and a liberal use of chrome. Just before World War II annual production was around 4000 units but unfortunately by 1959 it was all over for this quality truck builder from Detroit, Michigan.

Autocar was one of the few manufacturers which never stopped making cab-over-engine trucks. It had produced this type of commercial vehicle since they had gained popularity around 1915. Until well into the 1930s it produced a boxy flat-fronted model for contractors and builders who needed a rugged no-nonsense COE truck. These long-lived designs were not particularly handsome, but its successor of 1933, the US-Series, was a step in the right direction. Three years later it was followed up by the shapely UD-Series, and this successful cabover, which remained in production until Autocar was acquired by the White Motor Company in 1953, is regarded as a genuine classic.

Reo did not drop the production of passenger cars until 1936, but from then on it concentrated on building trucks and buses of which the most noteworthy pre-war design was the 'Speed Wagon'. They were reliable machines that also found ready acceptance in many markets abroad. A real classic appeared in 1949 when the stylish round nosed E-22 model was introduced. These conventional models with their unusual

Brockway has always built good looking, sturdy trucks. Here a smart 1935 Model 175X six-wheeler is loading beer barrels in Buffalo.

All-American Motor Freight Lines of Chicago used this Indiana Model 87 tractor in 1935 to pull a van type semi-trailer.

'nostril' grille design were powered by the famous 'wet sleeve' 6-cylinder 'Gold Comet' engine that later also became available in a LP-Gas conversion.

Before World War II Brockway was one of the largest truck makers in America, turning out over 5000 chassis annually. One of the most intriguing models in this company's history was the Model V1200 of 1934. Powered by a massive V-12 engine delivering 240hp, this was the most powerful truck of its day, but due to stringent (front) axle weight laws few of these monster trucks saw actual service. Although every single truck in the company's 65 year history was designed and built with pride and precision, some claim that the best Brockway ever was the Model 260. The long nosed 260 with its characteristic chrome radiator grille and large chromed headlights first appeared in the mid-1930s. It was equipped with a steel cab on a wooden frame, which Brockway kept in production until well into the 1950s by popular demand. It was argued that some drivers were afraid of getting trapped inside a steel cab, while a wooden structure would break up and free them in case of a severe accident.

In 1977 the name Brockway disappeared from the market when the Mack parent company decided to close the factory. And that brings us back to the Bulldog brand. Mack, according to some historians, produced the finest classic truck of all time: the B-model Mack. This high quality conventional with its four-point mounted steel 'comfort' cab of unitized construction and its smartly contoured hood and fender assembly, first hit the road on May 23, 1953. In a lifespan of over 13 years more than 130,000 B-models in various sizes and configurations were built. The handsome Bulldog became the envy of many a driver as it went about its business at home or abroad in the most diverse applications. With its powerful diesel engine it felt equally at home pulling a road train in Australia or delivering a load of fruit juice in downtown Philadelphia. Of course Mack was responsible throughout its long history for many more classic models, such as the beautiful LJ Diesel of the 1940s or the mighty LTSW West Coast 'long nose', but no other heavy truck can match the worldwide affection that the B-model Mack has aroused ever since its introduction some 45 years ago.

From 1936 to 1947
Labatt's Brewery in
Canada operated a fleet
of four different types of
'Streamliner', all based
on White COE tractor-
semitrailers with rather
futuristic bodywork by
Smith Bros of Toronto.

A rare sight is this stylish 1936 Mack 'cab-over-
engine' truck.. It could
very well be based on
the Mack Junior.

The 1930s were probably the most 'classic' years for Diamond-T. Styling, as seen on this 1936 Model 512DR six-wheeler, was so pleasing that it could only be matched by some automobiles.

In the second half of the 1930s the 'cab-over-engine' design came back and this slippery Mack EMUT-model was even fitted with an integral sleeper.

Like others, White also adapted passenger-car styling to its trucks in the mid-1930s. Its aerodynamic designs were the creation of industrial ace Count Alexis de Saknoffsky.

▼ Just before the outbreak of World War II the Shell distributor in St Louis took delivery of this handsome White 800-Series COE, which pulled a set of Heil trailerized tanks of 3500 and 2800 gallon capacity.

For a few decades, Sterling was a much heralded truck maker producing really 'macho' trucks such as this Model HD tractor with integral sleeper.

Another great Diamond-T classic from 1940. The heavy-duty Model 806 differed from lighter models by having a slightly less rounded radiator-grille and different hood louvers.

The big Mack Model EQ was made from 1937 to 1950 and was admired by many for its beautiful lines and unparalleled reliability.

Autocar never stopped making what is called 'engine-under-seat' trucks after its first such design had appeared in 1908. This tough looking Model UTD dates back to 1939.

This late 1930s Sterling Model JC137H with its long hood and intriguing iron grille-work operating in California had quite a striking appearance.

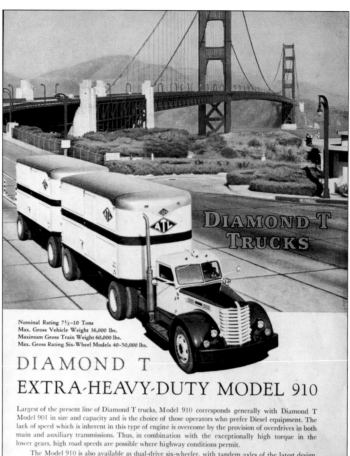

Diamond-T trucks, big or small, looked really handsome. The cab design was not their own, being for many years made by coach-builder McLaughlin.

Nominal Rating 7½–10 Tons
Max. Gross Vehicle Weight 36,000 lbs.
Maximum Gross Train Weight 60,000 lbs.
Max. Gross Rating Six-Wheel Models 40–50,000 lbs.

DIAMOND T
EXTRA-HEAVY-DUTY MODEL 910

Largest of the present line of Diamond T trucks, Model 910 corresponds generally with Diamond T Model 901 in size and capacity and is the choice of those operators who prefer Diesel equipment. The lack of speed which is inherent in this type of engine is overcome by the provision of overdrives in both main and auxiliary transmissions. Thus, in combination with the exceptionally high torque in the lower gears, high road speeds are possible where highway conditions permit.

The Model 910 is also available as dual-drive six-wheeler, with tandem axles of the latest design.

Voted a top classic by many is the Mack LJT with its long hood and 'ears' on the fenders. Harris operated this beautifully executed sleepercab tractor with Cummins diesel and Fruehauf van trailer on its southern express services in the 1940s.

A Federal Model 65M2 with integral sleeper and Brown reefer trailer pictured in Chicago in 1948. Like Diamond-T, heavy-duty Federals could be distinguished from lighter models by the more angular radiator grille and higher hood line.

In a way, this aluminum bodied heavy-duty Diamond-T truck and trailer looks like a typical long haul rig in the West. But it is not. This is a classic example of how European operators used to convert ex-US Army trucks into slow but reliable civilian wagons after World War II.

Reo introduced the round nosed E-Series in 1949. It was an immediate success, partly due to its trusty Gold Comet engine.

Heavy-duty trucks had proved their worth during the War and although every third commercial vehicle on the road in 1953 was dated back to the 1930s, new ones like this diesel powered Autocar became the standard in long haul trucking.

The Mack LHT-model was launched in 1940 but serious production did not start until 1944. This brightly painted double hopper outfit was seen still operating in the Seattle area in 1958.

Pictured in California in 1956 is this double bottom Federal. During the war the company was best known for its heavy-duty wreckers, but an attractive range of civilian models appeared soon after.

When Sterling took over parts of the Fageol company just before the War, sales on the West Coast soon tripled. This old semi was still going strong in Washington-state around 1958.

The Diamond-T extra-heavy-duty Model 910N was launched in the mid-1940s. Its styling was clearly influenced by military truck design.

When the B-model was first introduced in 1953, nobody could foresee that it was going to become one of Mack's all time favorites, with of 73 different models in 13 years.

This is the third generation of the H-Series Mack 'Cherry Picker', which had a significantly lower and wider cab.

A concrete road in wintry Toledo forms the backdrop for this handsome Reo A-Series semi-van in March 1958.

A wonderful 1957 shot with pure-bred classics galore.

The heavy-duty Mack B-80 could easily be recognized by its tough angular steel fenders and a different radiator grille.

The Mack B-73 was a lightweight version for the West Coast. It had also a larger radiator to cope with hotter climates.

When White celebrated its Golden Anniversary in 1949, the all new 3000 COE was launched. With its aerodynamically styled hydraulic tilt cab it set new standards in COE trucking.

Although in smaller numbers than before the War, American heavy trucks were exported throughout the 1950s and '60s. This colorful Mack B-61 six-wheeler was photographed in 1975 in Barcelona, Spain.

From a distance the Diamond-T Model 831 with 'Comfo-Vision' cab was hard to distinguish from the International V-Series.

The big LTLSW Mack undoubtly has a place among the top classics. With its long angular hood and older L-Series cab, it looked well up to its task, which lay mainly in the Western states.

Nostalgia at its best in Detroit, 1958. The White Super Power with its long sleek hood and unusual radiator grille became a popular heavy-duty truck after the War.

On the restrictive highways of 1956 the new White 9000 with 90-inch BBC cab could offer a greater payload.

The Reo Model 30/31 was introduced in 1948, but although it looked good it was not very successful.

In 1953 Mack came out with a Kenworth 'Bull Nose' lookalike, designated the W-71. It was specially designed for the West Coast market.

Before 1967, when Diamond-T and Reo trucksbegan to be sold under the name Diamond-Reo, models like this Reo DCL COE already had many parts in common with Diamond offerings, because they were built in the same plant.

This aggressive looking Diamond-T 1000C COE dates from c.1966. It was short lived and actually an intermediate model between the earlier tilt-cab 921C and the later 931C COE.

Last cabover to appear from the Diamond-Reo stable in 1974 was the Royale II with its ornate radiator grille.

Instead of mounting a steel cab on its new Model 5000 in 1963, White designed an ultra-light cab that made generous use of aluminum and fiberglass.

White-cabbed Autocar with 90-inch BBC helped Autocar users to overcome new state maximum length limits in the early 1960s.

Like some other manu-
facturers, Diamond-T
sourced its tilt cab for
the 522C model from
International Harvester
in 1956.

The beautifully styled
Brockway Model 762
with 400hp Cummins
diesel engine was very
well able to pull a
Michigan train.

White introduced the angular 7000-Series cabover in the mid-1960s. It became very successful with large fleet owners.

When the Middle East oilfield boom was at its height, Kenworth developed a series of special offroad trucks. This Model 953 with its unusual twin radiator arrangement dates from c.1959.

Before Western Star separated from White when it was taken over by Volvo in 1982, the Canadian product was sold under the White Western Star badge. This 1970s rig is almost a classic.

Autocar has always been synonymous with good looking quality trucks, even when it became part of the White Motor Co. in 1954. This fine DC-Series oilfield rig operated in Wyoming.

THE LARGE VOLUME PRODUCERS

The Ford Model TT was basically a beefed up version of the T and in ten years over a million were built. This unusual rigid six-wheeler had a third steering axle and was converted by Jumbo in Holland.

This chapter deals predominantly with the commercial vehicles produced by the 'Big Three' (Ford, General Motors, Chrysler), as well as International Harvester, and Studebaker. These large volume- or mass-producers manufactured considerable numbers of a few basic models which were mostly derived from their passenger car range and also used variants of their engines. International Harvester is of course the exception as it never made cars but the company was, and in part still is, a manufacturer with an enormous scope, offering anything from tractors to buses and pickups to heavy trucks. Right from the start

in 1907 it produced vehicles in large numbers.

One of the reasons that the USA became a world leader in the production of commercial vehicles was the invention of the assembly line technique. The Ford Motor Company installed the world's first genuine truck assembly line at its Dearborn, Michigan, plant in 1914. This method of building motor cars was so quick that Ford ran into problems with the drying of the regular red, gray or green paint offered. Hence only one color became available from 1914 onwards, which was a special black paint imported all the way from Japan! Between 1908 and 1927 over 15

million Ford Model T cars and trucks rolled off the assembly lines. The 'Tin Lizzie', as this simple but sturdy Ford was called, became one of the most famous motor vehicles in history. Few people know, however, that Henry Ford did not intend to build a passenger car at all when he first started to experiment with motorized wagons. It is said that in his young days he dreamed of inventing some sort of motor driven vehicle that would make the life of a farmer who had to bring his products to market easier. The first vehicle that Henry Ford designed and built, around the turn of the century, was in fact a sort of delivery wagon. A more marketable version, the Model E, was launched in 1904 when the Ford Motor Company had been founded.

Although Ford built a commercial roadster and a van based on the Model T from 1911, these ex-factory models accounted for only a very small portion of the Ts that were used for early trucking duties. For example, in 1916 there were no less than 19 coachbuilders in the USA alone who offered stock model truck and bus bodies for the Model T. It was not until 1917 that Ford itself finally introduced a one ton truck chassis, the Model TT, which was basically a beefed up version of the T. It became an instant success and in ten years over a million were built. The commercial 'Tin Lizzie' was equipped with a strengthened and longer frame, lower gears and a worm drive rear axle. The 2.9 liter 4-cylinder engine and 2-speed transmission were taken over from the car range, although a good number of operators had an auxiliary 2-speed overdrive fitted for improved performance. In the early 1920s the Model TT became available with a fully closed cab and new pneumatic tires. By 1926 Ford had captured over 50 percent of the commercial vehicle market. Compare this with Chevrolet's less than two percent in the one ton segment and the enormous success of the Ford TT truck chassis is clear. This success was not restricted to North America, for the Model T conversions and the Model TT factory chassis became as popular overseas as on the home front. Because price and quality were partly dictated by the volume of production, mass-producers such as Ford and General Motors right from the start were very eager to find new markets for their wares abroad. After World War I, Ford became particularly strong in Great Britain, where for several years it had a total vehicle market share of around 40 percent.

In the 1920s the angular TT was replaced by the much more stylish Model AA and later the BB. In 1933 this was followed by the popular Ford V-8. These new models, with

GMC came into being in 1911 when General Motors' earlier acquired truck producers Rapid and Reliance were combined. This classic chain-drive tractor with early Fruehauf semi dates from 1918.

Before the War Studebaker offered a whole range of affordable truck models, often based on car designs. This tanker was delivered in 1927.

their crowned fenders and shapely sheet metal similar to passenger car styling of the day, helped Ford regain first place on the market again. After World War II one of the more significant models to appear was the bonneted F8 tractor of 1948, which featured a 145hp or 155hp V8 gasoline engine with a dual-throat carburetor, a heavy-duty 5-speed transmission with overdrive, hydraulic power brakes and power steering.

Chevrolet entered the commercial vehicle market with a one-tonner in the same year as its competitor, Ford. However, the T-Series, powered by a 3.7 liter 4-cylinder engine and a

In the late 1920s Ford replaced the angular Model T with the more stylish Model AA, which later became the BB. It became a popular work-horse in the USA and abroad, capturing a creditable 40 percent of the truck market in Great Britain for years!

3-speed transmission, never became as popular as the Model TT, selling only 2000 chassis in 1922. The R-Series, with enclosed cab and (optional) six wheels, introduced four years later, did rather better. In 1929 truck sales got another boost with the introduction of a new six-cylinder engine and a 4-speed transmission in the sturdy Chevrolet 6. It helped Chevrolet sell 60,784 trucks and buses in 1932. This was less than Ford at the time, but from 1933 onwards GM took the lead. Chevrolet and GMC trucks combined almost continuously outsold Ford until well into the 1960s. To increase market share in export countries GM factories were set up in Great Britain (1928) and in Canada (1930). The British factory later produced the well known Bedford brand, whose products were based on Chevrolet designs. In Canada Chevrolet trucks were built and sold for

▼ The GMC T85, T90 and T95 were the heaviest offerings from General Motors in 1932 with GVWs up to 40,000 pounds. They were also the most stylish models of the range.

many years under the name Maple Leaf. From 1934-36 Chevrolet designs incorporated a more stylish V-type radiator grille and a streamlined steel cab with low roof line. From then on its truck designs differed more in appearance from their passenger car designs.

Dodge came under the wing of Chrysler Motors in 1928. This is an early 1930s long haul tractor with sleepercab and two trailers.

En Serie Ford & Fordson
Vare & Lastvogne

marketed in the USA at all. With its forward tilting hood for easy maintenance and its good maneuverability the Chevrolet COE became a popular option for operators struggling with maximum length limits and tight urban traffic conditions.

Between 1936 and 1939 General Motors' Oldsmobile division also turned out a number of conventional and cab-over-engine trucks that were for export only. They were identical in appearance and specification to the Chevrolet and GMC offerings of the time, except for one model that was powered by a 3.8-liter 6-cylinder gasoline engine from the Oldsmobile car range. Quite a few Oldsmobile trucks found willing buyers in Belgium and Holland, where some were even converted to six-wheelers. This conversion was popular among Chevrolet truck users all over Western Europe, with the additional axle often being fitted by a local assembler.

General Motors was copying Chrysler's idea of 'badge engineering' trucks for export markets with its introduction of Oldsmobile medium-heavy trucks in the mid-1930s. These were sold through certain car dealers only. Chrysler had done the same with Dodge trucks, which were marketed as Fargo and DeSoto products abroad. Basically the latter models were just the same as Dodge truck offerings apart from some differences in the design of the radiator grilles and the hood ornaments. In Canada, heavy Fargo-badged Dodge trucks were popular right up to their demise on that market in 1972. Later, General Motors allowed clients the choice of whether to have their trucks badged Chevrolet or GMC, light- to medium-duty models coming off the Chevy assembly line and heavier trucks originating from GMC.

By 1926 Ford had captured over 50 percent of the commercial vehicle market, and like other mass producers it was anxious to find new markets. Colorful ads helped to achieve this aim.

Chevrolet did very well in export markets in the 1930s. The 'Montpelier' cabover model designed in 1937 was shipped abroad before being introduced on the home market a year later. A 77hp Hercules diesel engine that was also available in this 1.5 ton chassis was not

Overseas, American trucks were liked for their powerful engines, durability and good ride. This C-Line International was converted to a semi-forward control truck in Great Britain.

GMC saw the light of day in 1911 when General Motors combined its earlier acquired truck companies, Rapid and Reliance. Rapid, by the way, was one of the first makers of gasoline powered commercial vehicles to appear in America. During World War I GMC produced more than 21,000 commercial vehicles for the US Forces. Civilian production after the War centered around the K-Series, which was superseded in 1927 by the T-line. These good looking, sturdy trucks were an immediate success and by the early 1930s 10,000 chassis a year were being sold. The top of the range model was the impressive 15-ton T-95C six-wheeler, which, in combination with a GMC built three-axle trailer, found ready acceptance among Western operators.

In the 1930s GM was among the first manufacturers to design more streamlined commercial vehicles. It even had a special Art and Color department, which was responsible for the design of stylish aerodynamic cabs and truck bodies on the T-Series conventional and F-Series COE. In 1932 GMC was also one of the first makers to offer a factory installed integral sleeper on heavy trucks.

In 1938 total GM truck production surpassed the 50,000 mark and part of this annual output was powered by the frugal newly developed 2-cycle GM diesel engine. GMC liked to change the appearance of its commercial vehicles annually. Sometimes it was just a matter of modifying a radiator grille or adding some chrome, in other years completely new streamlined models were presented. The T/F-Series cabover for example, saw several style changes from boxy and square to almost round in less than five years. In the late 1930s General Motors reckoned that GMC buyers took a pride in their vehicles and hence a choice of dual-tone paint combinations were offered as standard.

During World War II civilian truck development stalled, but the GMC name became synonymous with sturdiness and quality due to the unparalleled battlefield achievements of the famous 2.5-ton 6x6 Cargo Truck of which no less than 562,750 were built. After the war these US Army surplus ACKW and CCKW models with their reliable 104hp 6-cylinder gasoline engines and soft-top or steel cabs found many good uses in numerous civilian duties around the world.

In the postwar years a complete new line of light-, medium- and heavy-duty trucks were

launched by General Motors as the GMC 100 to 900-Series. While the lighter pickup and van models closely resembled the Chevrolet offerings, the medium- and heavy-weight conventional and cabover trucks had a character more of their own. The stylish 'Cannonball' H/HD-Series COE became a popular choice in fleets and also among owner-operators. From 1954 onwards it was equipped with a 'service friendly' cab which offered much better access to the engine and driveline by using a clever system of folding seats and floorboards, and a counterbalanced engine cover. Apart from gasoline engines up to 232hp, the GMC 'bubblenose' could also be purchased with the new 6-71 Detroit Diesel delivering 200hp out of 6.9 liters. Today the 'Cannonball' GMC and the (heavy-duty)

This neat Dodge inspired 2.5-ton truck exported to Holland was one of the last models to bear the Graham Brothers badge. From 1929 on all trucks were known as Dodge Brothers.

The 1935 Ford truck models were characterized by a new grille, slanted louvers in the hood, and skirted front fenders. This V-8 powered tractor pulled a round-nosed Wilson van in Iowa.

conventional models with the same family signature have become wanted classics. Incidentally, Ford, GM and Dodge had been late starters in offering cab-over-engine designs, and it was not until 1938-39 that these large volume producers announced their COE models as an addition to their conventional line. Before that a few Ford and Dodge badged COEs were built by outside firms such as Montpelier using standard medium-duty chassis.

Dodge built its first commercial vehicles during World War I. Until 1924, however, most Dodge chassis emerged from the Graham Brothers plant, which had made a good business of converting car chassis into trucks and buses. In 1925 Graham Brothers became a division of Dodge, while in 1928 Dodge came under the wing of Chrysler Motors. Until 1935 all its trucks were badged 'Dodge Brothers' but after that date they were simply 'Dodge'. The company's most notable design in the mid-1930s was the Airflow tanker made for the Standard Oil Company and other oil firms. By 1940 the company had

built 265 of these smart streamlined integral tankers, based on a 4-ton capacity conventional truck chassis. A military classic evolved during and after World War II in the form of the 4x4 drive 1/2- to 3/4 ton 'Power Wagon'. This gasoline powered off-road truck was available as late as 1971 (for export) with many custom body styles. The 1973 'Big Horn' was one of the last 'classic' heavy-duty Dodge trucks. It was a massive looking conventional with a long fiberglass hood and the small cab with wraparound windshield that could also be seen on Dodge pickup trucks. Only 261 Big Horns were made in a little over two years

Studebaker was another mass producer that displayed a lot of auto-influenced designs in its trucks. Developing a commercial vehicle line has never been easy. However, a lot of the initial tooling costs could be saved by entering the truck and bus field with affordable models based on car designs. Throughout its first few decades Studebaker was particularly strong in commercial chassis for passenger coaches, hearses and ambulances. More serious truck production started in the early and mid-1930s with conventional and cabover models for payloads up to three tons. Some of these designs closely resembled the car line of the day. Studebakers were quite popular overseas too, partly due to their car-inspired ride qualities and powerful engines. As early as 1930 the company offered a truck model with a straight eight engine delivering 115hp. There was also a choice of 13 bodies of different height and length.

Like the other manufacturers, Studebaker was heavily involved in the production of trucks for the forces during World War II. The company built no less than 197,000 2.5 ton 6x4 and 6x6 cargo trucks, using a design similar to the famous GMC of the same capacity. When passenger car production was moved to Canada in 1964, the end of Studebaker's involvement in truck manufacture soon followed. In 1962 the company had still been good for the sale of 7400 medium to heavy trucks.

▼ With its slanted radiator grille and sleek fender line the K47 Dodge truck made a great looking Streamline tanker in 1934.

Canada has always closely followed the USA in the manufacture of cars and trucks. As early as 1922, the country managed to become the world's second largest producer of motor vehicles. Around this time the first Canadian-built International trucks appeared on the market. IHC has arguably given us the

▲ Despite financial problems in the years before, in 1936 Studebaker managed to come up with a stylish range of medium to heavy trucks powered by 6-cylinder Waukesha engines.

To give better load distribution and haul more weight this 1939 Chevrolet was equipped with an ACME third axle.

axles, although the new C-line with its characteristic V-type aluminum radiator grille in six-wheeler configuration was equipped with a Hendrickson tandem axle. In 1937 the company produced a fine classic, the D-line. These harmoniously styled conventional models had slanted V-windshields, pontoon fenders, roomy steel cabs with adjustable seats and soft cushions, more powerful engines and better brakes. Heaviest in the line up was the DRD-70 model that was powered by the Cummins HB-600 diesel engine developing 150hp.

During World War II IHC built more than 100,000 combat vehicles. The semi-military H-542 tractor became well liked in Western Europe as a trusty long distance hauler after the war. 1946 saw International's stylish pre-war K-line reappear with some modifications as the KB-range. With its all-steel safety cab, oversized hood with stainless steel radiator grille, and its mighty 200hp Red Diamond engine up front, the KBR-12 belonged to the cream of heavy-duty highway transportation.

Classic examples of International long haul models also appeared on the West Coast where the Emeryville plant turned out around 600 lightweight heavy-duty tractors and trucks a year from 1947 onwards. These impressive long-nosed Western Models were powered by Cummins 600 diesels or Hall-Scott gasoline or butane engines, and were offered with a wide range of other driveline options. In 1951 International sales reached

earliest example of a 'classic' commercial vehicle - the 'Auto Wagon'. The company built around 3500 of these 'highwheelers' with a small cargo body on the rear between 1909 and 1912. After the success of the simple but practical 'Auto Wagon', in 1915 IHC came up with a more conventional line of trucks, the Model F and H. Just like the Renault and Mack offerings around this time, the new Internationals had a rear-mounted radiator and a sloping hood. By 1921 IHC was producing approximately 7000 commercial vehicles annually, the majority in the one to five ton 'Speed' truck range. From 1934 onwards International manufactured its own

An unusual but stylish rig is this circa 1937 Ford six-wheeler with Heil milk tanker body. The Ford was converted to a COE by Transportation Engineers of Detroit.

160,980 units in the USA alone, which was partly attributable to the great success of the all-new L-line introduced in 1949. While the K-and KB-models were still basically an upgrade of the D-line, the new L-model was completely different from anything seen before. A major improvement over the old models was the wider 'Comfo-Vision' cab with a taller one-piece curved windshield. It offered a much better driver's environment in general due to a new cab and seat suspension techniques, less vibration and engine noise, and a much improved ventilation system. The cab was so well thought out that in the following years several other truck manufacturers started to build new models around the same structure, among them Diamond-T, Hendrickson, Reo, and half a dozen more. In 1953 the upper International range was extended with the R-line, which in looks was based on the popular light to medium L-models. The cab was the same and was manufactured again by the Chicago Mfg. Co. Until 1967 the R-line continued as one of IHC's most popular models .

And that brings us back to Ford which also built a truck cab that found its way into other manufacturers designs. In 1957 Ford Motor Co. introduced the C-Series low profile cabover. Although it was a rather modest looking design, the model lasted for an incredible 33 years. It surpassed the longevity records of any other car or truck produced, including the famous AC Mack and the Model T Ford. The C-Series cab was also fitted in a modified form to certain Mack, FWD and Hendrickson trucks for a while, with Ford owning the tools and controlling the sales of this legendary structure. Maybe the C-Series

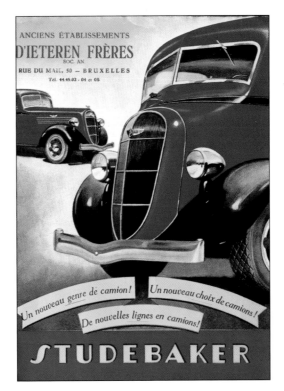

Before the War, Studebaker trucks and buses were exported to many countries. This colorful ad for the new 'Standard' Series appeared in Belgium around 1936.

as such is not a classic yet, but the top of the range H-Series COE tractors of 1961 which shared the same but heavily modified cab, certainly are.

From the 1930s to the 1960s, the products of the large volume producers like Ford, General Motors and Chrysler showed considerable design influence, both inside and out, from their parallel running passenger car lines. That it was the way to go can be seen by the fact that in 1962 alone sales of the combined volume producers totaled a mighty 350,000 medium- and heavy-duty trucks !

▼ In the mid-1930s General Motors started to make Chevrolet-based Oldsmobile trucks available to some car-only franchise holders in export markets. This Dutch conventional sports a locally built cab that follows the sleek hood and fender lines quite well.

In the early 1940s virtually every mass-producer offered a medium-heavy no-frills conventional that closely followed car designs of the time. The similarity in these pictures of Maple Leaf, GMC, Dodge and Fargo products is a good example. (picture a,b,c and d)

c

After World War II, many good uses were found for the trusty GMC ACKW and CCKW in numerous civilian duties around the world. This steel cabbed 6x6 was converted to a tractor-semitrailer rig.

In 1946 International's handsome pre-war K-Line reappeared with some modifications as the KB-model. This smart looking KB7 operated in Holland, pulling a locally built DAF trailer.

Ford introduced its distinctive F-range in 1948. Conventional and COE models included trucks with GVWs from 4700 to 21,500 pounds. They immediately sold well at home and abroad.

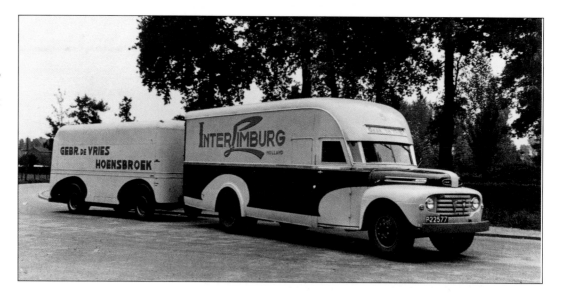

One of GMC's 1950s favorites was the 'Cannonball' H/HD-series COE. This diesel powered Model 620 spotted in 1957 in St Louis looks somewhat odd due to its altered 'bubblenose'.

▶ This classic GMC 900-Series conventional powered by a GM 6.71 diesel engine is seen with a box load of peaches in California around 1952.

◀ The tilt cab International DCO-405 was first seen in 1956. It was also built in Emeryville for West Coast operations and in 1959 received some minor styling changes including twin headlamps.

In some overseas countries American trucks just keep on going. This battered but complete 1947 Chevrolet COE was still at work in Uruguay in 1990.

Different length and weight laws created requirements for different trucks in the West. This long nosed Emeryville-built 1949 International W-Series had the two-man Fort Wayne type cab fitted.

In 1947 General Motors introduced an attractive new range of light to heavy 'Advance-Design' Chevrolet trucks. These 5000-Series COEs were used by the Antwerp gas company in Belgium.

This Ford Big Job F-800 tandem tractor with
Trailmobile tanker operated by Ecoff Trucking
made an impressive sight in 1957.

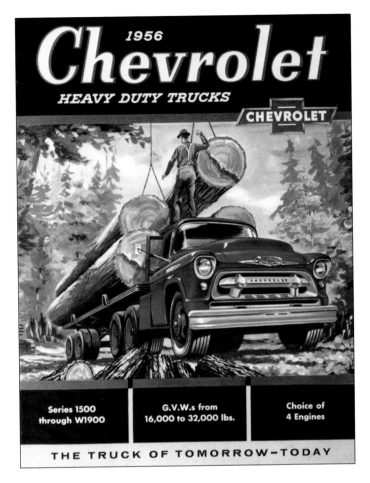

A colorful ad for the 1956 Chevrolet heavy-duty truck range. With the top of the range 322-cubic inch V8 engine of 215hp fitted this mass-produced truck proved a powerful workhorse.

The long nosed A-Series GMC was specifically designed in 1948 for use in Western states where axle spreads dictated overall gross weights.

International's western plant produced a few light weight COE tractors using the standard non-tilting W-Series cab in 1947. This rare W-3042-L tractor-semi with cramped sleeper pot was photographed in Chicago in 1957.

Another great shot of a classic Western International! This is a 1956 Model DC-405-L tractor with dromedary tank and trailers hauling sugar concentrate around San Francisco, California.

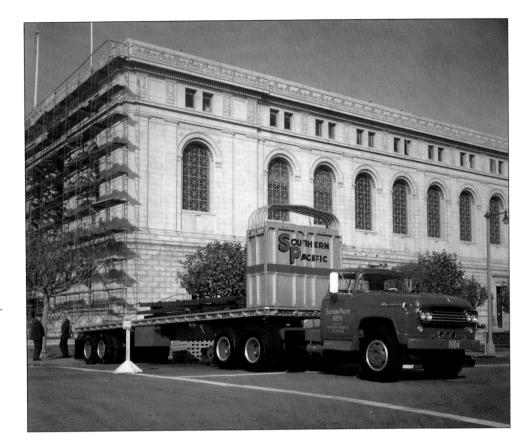

A quite handsome big rig was this gasoline-powered Ford T-800 Custom Cab tandem-axle job, hauling building materials in 1960 for Southern Pacific.

In 1953 the upper International range was extended with the R-Line, whose looks were based on the earlier L-Series using the same Chicago Mfg. Co. cab. This outstanding looking 1960s R-190 operated in Australia.

The Cab Forward
Chevrolet 5700 intro-
duced in 1956 had a
pleasing appearance
and the light, roomy
cab offered car-like com-
forts.

A classic 'Cannonball' GMC Model 630 COE with
slim-line cab and non-driven trailing axle pictured in
a wintry Wisconsin in 1955.

International was a major exporter after the war; these two sturdy diesel powered 6x6 R-190 models with Edbro dump bodies are seen working hard in Europe around 1966.

The 1964 angular styled GMC D-Series COE was generally known as the 'Crackerbox'. At least it had a 'face of its own', which could not be said of many of the other 1960s designs.

In 1959 Ford used its new C-Series Tilt Cab to produce this rare C-1000 lightweight cabover tandem tractor for Pacific Intermountain Express in California.

Another typical 1960s design is the boxy Dodge LN-1000 COE. It was a lightweight model with a large choice of engines and other mechanical options.

Although oilfield trucks have never been designed for good looks, they can certainly be impressive machines. This big RDF-320 saw service in 1966 around Nebraska.

zFrom the 1960s GM gave the customer the choice of having a truck badged as a Chevrolet or GMC. Hence models like this GMC Tilt Cab could also be ordered with minor modifications as the Chevrolet U80-Series.

One of the last classic heavy-duty Dodge trucks to appear was the 'Big Horn' in 1973. In two years only 261 of these massive machines were built.

Ford's short convention-al N-Series of the mid-1960s was also available in certain export mar-kets badged as a Mercury. This well kept tanker was spotted still working in Turkey in 1982.

A truly classic scene. These 1940s trucks were seen in 1996 fading quietly away in the Nevada desert near Tonopah.

THE WESTERN TRUCK MAKERS

Ever since the motor truck was recognized as a viable means of transporting all sorts of freight nearly a century ago, drivers and operators have shown preferences for particular makes. These can be dictated by loyalty for a brand or dealer in the neighborhood, the type of the freight hauled, the purchase and service price, or geographic conditions. Although geographic preference for certain makes is less acute than say 30 or 40 years ago, even today truckers in and around the big cities in the East are in general more inclined to buy a Ford, Mack or Volvo (White), which are built in their area, than a product from one of the manufacturers out West. Of course there is still a substantial difference in legislative and operating conditions between the East and the West, and this also influences the design of vehicles and the choice of equipment made by the users. On the other hand, Western truck manufacturers have adapted their products remarkably well in recent years to

the varying needs of truckers in the East. As a consequence, typical West Coast products such as Freightliner and Kenworth are now almost as common on the streets of New

The Kenworth name first appeared in 1922 when owners H.W. Kent and E.K. Worthington started to use a combination of their names to adorn the new 'Gersix' truck product.

A 7-speed Fageol seen in the early 1920s hauling a heavy load through the jungle of South-East Asia in the presence of a large audience.

Moreland was a pacesetting West Coast truck manufacturer which between 1911 and 1941 produced many fascinating conventionals. Pictured is a big R-Series six-wheeler from around 1936 with very pleasing looks.

York as in Los Angeles. But although the brand name on the hood may be the same, the unit itself can differ a lot in specification. Where Western rigs make extensive use of lightweight aluminum components and air ride suspension, emphasis in the East is on heavy-duty construction. Depending in which state and to what legislative requirements they are operating, more or less axles, lift devices, varying axle spreads, and longer tow bars are fitted.

Eighteen-wheelers that run from coast to coast are different again. Such long haul trucks must be specified very carefully because they have to comply with varying state laws. There is no great visible difference

between a rig hailing from Oregon or Florida, apart from the number of cosmetic options fitted and the fancy paint that may be applied. This sort of glamor is usually more prominent on West Coast rigs than on the trucks of the more conservative Eastern hauliers. In California even fleet trucks can be seen adorned with chrome goodies and cabs or bodywork executed in bright metallic paint jobs. For many owner operators it is a way to express their individuality. Customizing was first seen on the West Coast before World War II, when owners of valuable passenger cars were looking for ways to impress others on the road even more. In the 1950s this phenomenon was taken over by the truck men, and soon after virtually all Western truck manufacturers offered some sort of customized 'owner operator special' fitted with lots of accessories and fancy paint work.

Due to the elaborate use of optional extras and the differing weight and length laws, trucks west of the Rockies have always had a flavor of their own, yet for years the basic design of these trucks changed very little. Notably, Kenworth and Peterbilt clung for a very long time to massive conventional models incorporating a long nose and narrow radiator grille, with the headlights mounted on the side of the hood rather than on the fenders. A V-type windshield and small side

windows in a rather cramped and angular steel or aluminum cab were also typical design features of these uninspiring but very durable trucks. Even today most Western manufacturers offer at least one long-nosed truck model that reflects the lines of the basic design that was adopted way back in the 1940s, albeit with an up-to-date specification underneath. This new 'classic' breed is aimed at the discerning owner operator who wants a truck that combines excellent ride qualities, low fuel consumption, and a durable construction with the macho appearance from the old days.

Although West Coast manufacturers and operators now lead the nation on many fronts, they were not at all progressive earlier in the century. In the early 1920s when the motor truck was gaining considerable ground as a means of freight transport in other parts of America, the majority of Western operators still preferred the old horse and wagon. The weather and terrain in this part of the country obviously differed a lot from the more civilized states in the East, but the thing that really stalled motorization in the West was that operators there were reluctant to try and use the 'toy trucks' manufactured east of the Rockies. They argued that the Eastern products were not strong enough to withstand the rigors of hauling heavy loads over unmade tracks through snow covered mountains and

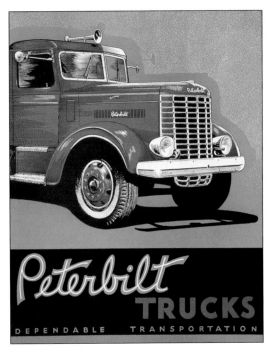

In April 1939 lumberman T.A. Peterman of Tacoma, Washington, purchased the Fageol make. The first Peterbilt truck, a Model L-100 six-wheeler, rolled out of the factory doors on August 2.

blistering hot deserts. And so thought the brothers Edgar and Louis Gerlinger in Portland, Oregon. They were prominent northwestern railroad and lumber men, but they also had a flourishing business selling cars, vans and trucks. The latter included Federal products, which were modified locally for hard use in the West. In 1916 this lead to the development of a truck of their own named the Gersix. It was a 3 ton affair

The 1937 Fageol was more streamlined but retained the unusual louvers on the top of the hood. This model was later to become the basis of Peterbilt designs.

◀ An incredible view from the past! This 1935 long haul Kenworth with integral sleeper sports lots of optional equipment, as seen on big trucks many decades later.

These intriguing models with their pontoon style fenders and very attractive hood and cab lines were also made by Kenworth in the mid-1930s.

largely based on the Federal design but now powered by a big 6-cylinder Continental engine instead of the four-pot Federal unit. It was no easy time to start in the truck manufacturing business with World War I going on and all sorts of materials in short supply. After a year of muddling through in Portland, Tacoma and Seattle, only a handful of trucks had been completed. In 1917 the assets were sold to three Seattle businessmen, H.W. Kent, E.K. Worthington and F.A. Keen. The new Gersix Manufacturing Company did better and truck number 42 was sold before the end of that same year.

By 1922 truck design and production had progressed to such an extent due to the dedication of the Seattle owners that a new name was being sought for the products. It became 'Kenworth', which is a combination of the names Kent and Worthington. Right

from the start Kenworth adhered to the custom built approach, producing exactly what the customer asked for and in general tailoring trucks better to fit the special needs of trucking in the tough conditions of the Pacific Northwest. Due to the incorporation of a new driveline with a 4-cylinder Buda engine and a 4- or 7-speed transmission, Kenworth managed to sell 159 trucks in 1926. For severe winter operation, the company was also quick to offer such 'luxuries' as a fully enclosed cab, and with huge mountain ranges all around, much thought went into the development of better braking systems.

In 1932 Kenworth was the first truck manufacturer to install a 100hp Cummins diesel engine ex-factory. In combination with a 4- and 3-speed dual transmission these new diesels could easily surpass the performance of the popular 672 cubic inch gasoline powerplants with no appreciable increase in size or weight. Nevertheless the big gasoline and butane fueled engine would not leave the West Coast truck scene until late in the 1940s and in 1933 some Kenworths were equipped with butane gas powerplants that were said to improve miles per gallon by a good 25 percent over normal gasoline units.

Until the mid-1930s most of the Kenworth cab construction was done by Heiser Body to specifications laid down by the factory, but 1935 the company started to build its own cabs. The first design remained in production almost unchanged for nearly 25 years, although there was a fair bit of customizing. Characteristic was the front-end design with the slanted radiator grille and chrome tubes, still recognizable in some conventional models produced as late as the 1970s.

Peterbilt produced 14 trucks in 1939. These Model 260 trucks with the distinctive chrome grille were delivered to the Union Sugar Co. of Oakland.

A 'no-name conventional' modified by Consolidated Freightways in 1941. This was the forerunner of the much later Freightliner conventional.

In 1950 the Hyster Company became the first private carrier to buy a Freightliner tractor. This Model 900 was the first long haul Freightliner with an integral sleeper.

To comply with new length laws Kenworth introduced its first cab-over-engine model, the 516, in 1936. It was a rather angular design with set-back front axle, and in 1939 a more rounded model appeared that had a larger cab mounted higher on the chassis. After World War II production of these lightweight COE highway trucks continued until in 1948 its successor, the 'Bull Nose', was introduced. This square-nose design which used several parts of the Kenworth conventional model such as roof and door, remained in production until 1956. The 'Bull Nose' was available with a day cab or integral sleeper structure made of heavy steel. Hence it was certainly not a lightweight job, but

▼ From 1944 on Peterbilts like this Model 344 were adorned with a new badge that showed the 'Peterbilt' name on a rectangular base on both the grille and the hood sides.

A smart round-nosed Kenworth COE fitted with one of the first separate sleepers, a new idea in 1947.

due to its impressive appearance and good engineering it became a popular choice among long haul truckers. Today it is regarded as one of the finest classics Kenworth ever built.

From 1950 onwards Kenworth was very active in the development and construction of ultra heavy-duty 6x6 drive truck chassis for the world's oilfield industries. For the Saudi-Arabians, Kenworth built no less than 1700 special Hall-Scott and Cummins powered off-highway tractors in the 1950s for operation at weights up to 300 tons across virgin desert. The big Model 953 Super with its characteristic V-shaped radiator grille, huge sand tires, extremely strong chassis and diesel engines up to 600hp has become a

legend in oilfield trucking around the world.

By 1952 annual production at Kenworth had reached the 1000 mark, and the most popular model was the 'Needle Nose' conventional, introduced in 1940. On this truck the slanted grille gave way to a more upright design. It was to be a Kenworth hallmark for many years to come until 1961, when the W900 conventional with wider fiberglass tilt hood started to make inroads.

The roots of another Paccar subsidiary, Peterbilt Motors Co., can be traced back to the drawing boards of the pre-war Fageol Motor Car Company of Oakland, California. Fageol had set up a manufacturing business for luxury automobiles and tractors in 1915, but from the early 1920s on concentrated solely

Peterbilt sold 316 units in 1948. The Model 270 had a rounded radiator and steel bumper with four holes in it, which on later models was replaced by one with horizontal slots.

on the production of commercial vehicles. The company soon earned a reputation for building rugged and reliable heavy-duty four- and six-wheel trucks that were well suited for long hauls across the steep mountain ranges of the West Coast. In 1929 Fageol was one of the first to experiment with aluminum frame rails and light alloy cab parts. Its conventional bus and truck models could be easily recognized by the unusual row of finned ventilators adorning the top of the hood. In 1930 a merger with another Western truck manufacturer, Moreland, was proposed, but because of Fageol's weak state at the time the deal never materialized. Moreland was a relatively small West Coast manufacturer but its products were technically advanced with six-wheelers, diesel power and light weight construction already offered in the mid-1920s. By 1930 Moreland was building nearly 1000 units a year, including trailers and truck bodies. A real classic was the Model R Series of 1936 with its rounded hood and fender lines and roomy cab with V-shaped windshield. It was available in six capacities up to a weight of 30,000 pounds. Three gasoline engines were offered, as well as Moreland's own straight-six diesel and units from Hercules or Cummins. Even disc brakes were listed as an option!

Compared to the boxy designs of other Western truck products the Moreland was way ahead of its time and was impressive from whatever angle you looked at it, but during World War II the company's truck and bus production came to a virtual halt and in 1949 the assets were taken over by Cook Brothers.

Fageol in the meantime came out with a new more streamlined cab and a cab-over-engine model in 1937, but the company also faced stiff financial problems just before the war, resulting in a buy out by Sterling in

When Freightliner signed a sales and service agreement in 1951 with the White Motor Co., products appeared with the 'White-Freightliner' nameplate on them.

trucks produced had risen to 349 for the year. The unusual front end was changed, but it was not until 1949 that an all-new model was launched. With its tall narrow hood and a flat radiator grille the Peterbilt Model 280 and 350 looked quite similar to the Kenworth 'Needle Nose' of the 1950s. In 1950 the first Peterbilt cabover was introduced: the Model 350 COE with its stylish snub-nosed front end was soon called a 'Bubble Nose' by operators. A tilt cab model, it was made until 1956 and became notably popular with West Coast operators trying to squeeze every inch out of the new overall length limitations.

Kenworth's classic 'Bull-Nose' COE was introduced in 1948 and became an instant success among long haul truckers.

This great 1945 Peterbilt Model 334 with Timpte refrigerated trailer was painstakingly restored by its Californian owner.

1938. A year later truck production ceased and the plant and property were taken over by T.A. Peterman, a Western logging contractor who renamed the company 'Peterbilt'. With a model based on the last Fageol design, Peterbilt Motors Company produced only 14 truck chassis and one fire engine in its first year. The conventional featured a rather square cab matched to a long contoured hood and a strange cast-aluminum radiator grille. Being himself well aware of the heavy loads and difficult conditions that faced logging operators in the Pacific northwest, T.A. Peterman concentrated on building durable models for on- and off-highway use, and by 1949 the number of

This classic was superseded by the more flat fronted Model 351, which in 1959 made way again for the third generation cabover, the renowned Model 352. Peterbilts were (and still are) custom built, and due to the incorporation of aluminum cab and frame parts often weighed up to 2000 pounds less than trucks from the competition. In the classic years, Peterbilt Motors Co. was a forerunner in the development and use of air-suspension, planetary axles, a 90 degree tilt cab, the 'top sleeper', and the 'dromedary box'. The latter consisted of an extra freight compartment fitted behind the cab of a long wheelbase tractor and was developed in conjunction with P.I.E. to increase versatility in the line hauling of light goods.

From the start, Western states required a

Los Angeles Seattle Motor Express operated this classic Model 350 Peterbilt COE with aluminum bodywork and trailer on long haul duties in the 1950s.

different type of truck where payload volume was more important than the ability to carry heavy loads. Liberal length regulations allowed the use of three-axle truck and trailer combinations, but weight limitations made the incorporation of light-alloy materials a necessity.

Another line haul carrier which experimented a lot with lightweight maximum length trucks in the 1930s and 1940s was Consolidated Freightways of Portland, Oregon. Its founder and director, Leland James, was also in a way responsible for the current number one US truck manufacturer, Freightliner. James, however, initially did not want to go into truck production at all. He simply wanted a durable truck that could haul more legal payload than the existing vehicles in his fleet. Throughout the 1930s Consolidated Freight Lines, as it was then known, modified trucks and built trailers and truck

Due to its low tare weight and custom build specification the sleeper cabbed (White) Freightliner COE became a popular long haul truck among Western carriers in the 1950s.

This impressive long wheelbase eight-wheeler with 'pancake' engine and aluminum panelled dromedary box was built by Kenworth in 1956 for P.I.E.'s demanding Western intercity hauls.

bodies of aluminum. In 1937 a 4x2 Fageol conventional was turned into a COE truck and refitted with a more powerful Cummins diesel. It was not a thing of beauty and soon got the nickname 'Monkey Ward' because it looked as if it had been assembled from mail-order parts. Around 20 were built before it was decided in 1940 to set up a truck manufacturing business in Salt Lake City under the name of Freightways Mfg. Company. That year nine lightweight COE trucks were produced using bought-in parts

from Alcoa, Cummins, Eaton, Fuller and Rockwell. Although a few more trucks, badged as a 'Freight-Liner', were built in 1941, shortages of labor and materials during the war and legal disputes forced the young company to close in 1944.

In 1947 some of the original staff started up again in Portland. The 'Freightliner' Model 800 'Bubble Nose' with an all-new aluminum cab was born. With its many lightweight parts and high payload volume the truck was an instant success in the CF fleet, so much so that it was soon decided to sell the Freightliner COE to third parties, starting with a unit to produce haulier Vince Graziano in 1948. The first sleepercab version Model 900 sold to a private carrier went to the Hyster Company in 1950. It was America's first COE tractor with an integral sleeper and Freightliner's first truck with a 10-speed transmission. The Hyster 'Bubble Nose' clocked up an amazing four million miles in its working life and this true classic can now be seen in the Smithsonian Museum in Washington.

During the early 1940s Freightliner also tried its hand at the design of a conventional model, but this only appeared as a no-name truck in CF's own fleet. The uniquely styled

This pristine looking Kenworth 'Bull-Nose' with short BBC cab was delivered to Mobilgas in California in 1952. Note the re-located hardware behind the cab and the protective shield over the exhaust pipe.

'Bubble Nose' was superseded in 1953 by a more angular COE model with a riveted aluminum cab that offered new standards in ride and driver comfort. An even more refined 'White Freightliner' saw the light in 1958 as the Model WF. It received a new radiator grille and became the industry's first tilt-cab aluminum COE. Annual sales were rising rapidly and reached 14,344 units in 1974. A year later the marketing agreement with White ended and Freightliner remained independent until Daimler-Benz took over in 1981. Since then Western truck manufacturers, with Freightliner in the forefront, have made tremendous inroads not only in sales of trucks on their home ground, but also in sales of premium trucks to owner-operators and fleets in other parts of North America and even on some export markets.

The typical styling of a 1950s conventional long haul truck is shown to advantage in this colorful picture of a 'narrow-nosed' Kenworth loading up in Seattle around 1958.

Another classic relic from the past is this Kenworth Model 523 COE operating for Western Tank Lines in Washington state.

The odd looking CBE (Cab-Beside-Engine) Kenworth was designed in 1953 for use on mountain passes in the West.

The much more flush-fronted Model 351 with 'Panoramic Safe-T-Cab' was launched by Peterbilt in 1955 and replaced the short-lived 'Bubblenose' a year later.

A big 290 Hall-Scott gasoline engine was mounted under the uniquely shaped hood of this 1949 Hayes logging truck.

Freightliner was never afraid of building one-off rigs for clients, such as this modified WF-5844T tractor for Spector in 1955.

Basically it consisted of two double vans with the lead trailer coupled rigidly to the tractor for long haul transfer.

In the late 1940s Peterbilt introduced a new generation of conventionals that was easily recognized by its tall radiator. This Model 280 pulled a double hopper train in California.

A fine example of a 1956 vintage Kenworth 'Bull-Nose' sleeper tractor, packed with options and pulling a Brown refrigerated semitrailer for Rayette of St Paul.

Freightliner's WF-Series with the industry's first 90 degree tilt cab was a major leap forward in 1958. Due to its success the 10,000th Freightliner was built in 1963.

The postwar 'Needle Nose' Kenworth made an impressive Western long haul truck. This classic Model 523 was photographed in 1958 near Mt Vernon in Washington.

The Canadians have built many remarkable trucks. Just witness this beautifully kept Hayes Conventional Clipper of 1963.

A replacement for the classic 'Bull-Nose' appeared in 1954 in the form of the Kenworth CSE (Cab-Surrounding-Engine) type. It had a more flat-fronted design and was the forerunner of the K100 COE.

Kenworth set up a branch factory in Vancouver in 1929 producing specific models for the Canadian market. This early 1950s classic was still hauling hard in 1991.

In the 1950s chromed extras and fancy paint jobs came into being. Although a bit dirty, this Freightliner's owner-operator has tried hard to make his truck stand out from the crowd.

With a tall narrow hood and a flat radiator grille Peterbilt conventionals of the 1950s looked quite similar to Kenworth designs of the time.

Another classic from north of the border. The Hayes Clipper 200 with its characteristic hood and grille had a true 'face of its own' and was introduced in 1970.

Although not (yet) a classic, the Pacific P-500-F with its Paystar 5000 cab, fiberglass hood and typical air-cleaner had a distinctive style when launched in 1977.

This high cabover Kenworth was the prototype for the so successful later Aerodyne. In 1974 it was sent to Alaska for road testing for a year.

SMALLER MANUFACTURERS

Throughout the 1930s and '40s hundreds of thousands of American trucks found a willing buyer in markets abroad. The majority of these vehicles were shipped in so called CKD-form (Completely Knocked Down), which means that they were packed in crates and assembled in the country of destination. Sometimes the trucks or buses would be virtually identical to the ones used in the USA, at other times the finished product would contain many local parts including major items such as the engine and cab. Shipping costs prohibited shipping fully built-up vehicles overseas or packing too many large parts in a crate, so in export markets bodywork was mostly obtained from local suppliers. A powerful and durable American chassis married to a sophisticated European cab enabled many exporters to offer a well built and competitively priced vehicle. Interestingly, it was not only the large manufacturers who had trucks assembled abroad. Many smaller makers, from Condor to Stewart and Republic to Willys, were at one time or another active in the assembly of truck and bus chassis in specific overseas markets. Literally hundreds of US manufacturers have tried their hand at exporting their products. Many were successful, others failed — over the years scores of smaller producers did not make the grade on their home ground either. Since the turn of the century nearly 1850 truck makers have tried to get established, but many did not make it further than a few years or at best a decade or two. Only manufacturers who had acquired full knowledge of all the requirements of in truck design and transport legislation in the 1930s managed to survive and succeed after the War and beyond. These were also the firms who were able and willing to design and build heavy trucks for particular needs and give

In the early days scores of smaller producers tried to establish themselves. Between 1910 and 1928 no less than four different manufacturers of Victor commercials were active on the American market.

An 8-ton worm-drive six-wheeler of around 1929 vintage built by the Chicago Motor Truck Co. It still had solid tires, but also a fully enclosed cab with raked windshield.

Another rarity is the Krebs, produced for only three years in Ohio by the Krebs Motor Truck Co. This 1924 3-tonner was powered by a Continental engine.

components as possible. These were either made in-house or bought in, but in practice they were not always perfectly compatible, and as a consequence some weird contraptions evolved that may have done their job well but were a headache to drive. Notably some of the smaller manufacturers often forgot that a truck could only be operated efficiently when the man behind the wheel was feeling at ease. Large volume producers building trucks that offered car-like driver comforts certainly had the edge and for small makers particularly the design and construction of draught-free steel cabs and quiet, powerful gasoline engines proved a problem in the 1930s. While engine and driveline components could easily be bought in, the cab was often the deciding feature in the design, hence smaller makers sometimes

A beautiful example of a Massachusetts built Netco truck from the mid-1920s. The company made a small number of 1.5- to 7-ton trucks between 1914 and 1938.

operators exactly what they wanted.

Many smaller makers have failed over the years because they could not maintain sufficient production numbers to cover the high costs of design and manufacture. The models they offered were generally of high quality and handbuilt, hence expensive. A solution was to use as many standard

This Gotfredson stake truck looked quite smart in 1933 with its long hood, stylish wooden cab and two-tone paint scheme.

For some years LeMoon built a utilitarian range of trucks. This Model HG30 with 1000 gallon aluminum tank by GarWood was photographed in 1934.

had tremendous difficulty in competing with the established manufacturers due to a lack of sophistication in the ride and cab comfort of their products. Nevertheless, some smaller producers managed to compete in the market with beautifully made trucks that were the envy of many a larger company. These were mostly tailor-made products meant for niche markets that were either overlooked or ignored by the mass producers. With their low operating overheads due to the absence of big design and production

Attention to detail was superb in this sturdy looking N-Series American-LaFrance of 1925. It was fitted with a 1800 gallon three-compartment Heil tank.

In 1932 the 1.5-ton Republic Fleetmaster was a truck 'with a distinctive appeal and beautiful yet sturdy lines' according to the sales literature.

There were strong links between Gramm and Willys from 1927 to 1930. In addition to Gramm's own line of stylish trucks, such as this 1931 8-ton sleepercab tractor, they also built Willys Six models for export markets.

departments and to more simple assembly techniques, and with a thorough knowledge of their customers' needs, some smaller makers became quite successful in specific segments of the industry.

In contrast to most large volume producers, who redesigned their car based truck ranges almost annually, the smaller makers had to do with a new model once in a decade. Like the larger 'independent' manufacturers, smaller producers of heavy-duty trucks had to look closely at reducing engineering costs and simplifying manufacture. To permit maximum production at minimum cost the design of parts had to be focused on standardizing dimensions wherever possible. In this way even smaller firms were able to come up with a competitively priced heavy truck that in many cases offered more variations in specification than the products from the larger established manufacturers. Another telling factor in the success of some smaller firms was that whereas the large volume producers offered mostly trucks based on the styling of their passenger car ranges, the smaller-scale firms designed the 'real' thing. That is, 'trucks that looked like trucks'. It took until the 1950s before some of the mass producers started to offer genuine truck models by developing new dies and thus distinguishing this segment more from their automobile designs. Commercial vehicles in the lowest weight categories, however, remained based on passenger car chassis.

Virtually all the smaller truck makers only made light- to medium-weight vehicles at the outset. In the 1920s a 4-ton truck was considered a heavy-duty model and the bulk of commercials used had a payload capacity of between one and three tons.

In 1922 there were no less than 242 different US-manufacturers trying to earn a buck building commercial vehicles. Only a few were successful enough to stay in business for a prolonged period, and most smaller makers had disappeared by the end of the 1930s. Many simply stopped manufacturing heavy trucks, while some were taken over by rivals, some were merged with other small companies, and some just disappeared. After World War II, the strongest and most innovative firms were quick to take up the manufacture of new trucks again, sometimes only to find themselves in turn taken over by yet larger concerns, notably during the 1950s and '60s when competition became really cut-throat in the upper weight class.

Another fine make was Schacht. This early 1930s long wheelbase horse van with its over-cab rack looks fit for its task.

A rare, beautifully restored 1928 Maccar Model 66 removal van. The make came about when Jack Mack, one of the Mack brothers, and Roland Carr set up their own truck company in 1912.

The Pierce-Arrow badge appeared on vehicles other than the firm's exclusive cars. This classic 12,000 pound GVW Model PT tractor-semi was delivered to the New England Co. in 1932.

A late-1930s view of the small assembly-line at Brown Truck & Equipment Co. in Charlotte, N.C., where half a dozen classic conventionals for Horton Motor Lines are being built.

When times are lean, smaller manufacturers are often hard hit because they lack a broad truck range and are not selling their product nationwide due to their limited distribution network. In general the products from smaller truck makers are confined to the area in which they are built. Apart from a number of specialist manufacturers dealt with in another chapter of this book, hardly any smaller truck makers have survived into the 1990s. Of the hundreds of small producers that were active in the past, the only one still making trucks untill a year ago

and worth mentioning here is Marmon — and even this Texas-based producer of premium highway trucks was merely a distant descendant of another US company, the once famous Marmon-Herrington special equipment manufacturer.

To broaden its product range Marmon-Herrington had developed an all new highway tractor just before its collapse in 1963. When the assets were sold to a distributor in Garland, Texas, this firm also acquired the plans to build the new COE trucks and market them under the Marmon name. The first models to appear from the new Marmon Motor Co. were the HDT-86 sleeper COE and the HDT-51 non-sleeper tractor. They were custom built jobs of boxy design using many all-aluminum cab and frame parts. Power options included Cummins, Caterpillar or Detroit Diesel, while transmissions came from Fuller or Spicer and axles were Eaton or Rockwell. A custom-built conventional with the same varied specification was added within a year as the Model CHDT. This rather angular shaped truck with its big bold fiberglass hood has always been a rarity but in a way it is a classic too. Marmon-Herrington's most intriguing truck models appeared in the 1930s, when several giant 6x6 off-highway tractors were built for arduous oilfield duties and long distance bus operations in the deserts of the Middle East and North Africa.

As has been noted, by the 1970s virtually all smaller makers had disappeared from the

One of the lesser known makes is Reiland-Bree. In the 1930s this company built a small number of typical medium and heavy trucks like this sturdy six-wheeler with twin-ram hoist and body by Heil.

In the 1930s a good number of smaller manufacturers were active in exporting and assembling truck and bus chassis in various countries abroad. This smart Stewart with locally made cab and DAF semitrailer operated in Europe.

When in 1929 American-LaFrance's truck division merged with the Republic Motor Truck Company, new products appeared with the LaFrance-Republic badge on the hood.

North American highway truck market, so to look for 'classic' heavy trucks from small makers we have to go back much further, for example to Brown, which appeared in 1939 when the Charlotte, North Carolina,. based carrier Horton Motor Lines started to build highway equipment for its own use. The truck was named after its engineer and designer J.L. Brown and was built until 1953 as a conventional and cabover. Although they were partly built in aluminum to save weight the Brown was a very rugged truck that found ready acceptance among buyers from 1942 onwards, and considering the small production run of just over 1000 units in 14 years, it was a pretty good-looking design too that rightly deserves the 'classic' label.

Another long forgotten company that produced some fine classic truck models was the Available Truck Co. of Chicago. The first

truck from this manufacturer was a 3/4-ton model in 1910. More significant models were seen in the 1930s, including cab-over-engine designs and a number of six-wheelers, primarily powered by Waukesha gasoline engines or diesels by Buda and Cummins. In 1934, Available 'Tractor Models' could according to a company leaflet be had with 'hand-built sleeper cabs at moderate prices which include windshield wiper, rear-view mirror, 26-inch bed, locks on the doors and domelight'. Three years later the streamline craze had also reached the drawing office of this small Chicago manufacturer and a full line of slippery COE trucks in the 1.5 to 10 ton class was launched. A handsome range of conventional truck models, the X-Series, was available in the same weight category and to a similar specification. During the 1940s the flat fronted WS-Model was superseded by the CS-Series, which had a more rounded appearance, while the new conventionals became the handsomely styled C-Series, now offered with 'Deluxe 3-man cab' as standard. Despite the incorporation of many quality engineering features and considerable investment in a modern and appealing design, actual production numbers remained low throughout Available's 47 years of existence as a heavy-duty truck builder.

In Buffalo, New York state, from 1912 onwards another well known smaller truck manufacturer started to make headlines: the Stewart Motor Corporation. By 1918 its range included truck and bus models up to 3.5 tons capacity which came with a wide choice of

This Cummins powered Gotfredson with stylish cast aluminum radiator and GMC cab is hauling a full load in Michigan in 1938.

▶
A real classic is this early 1930s Grass-Premier special tractor, seen pulling four dump wagons for the City of Madison, WI. It was powered by a 6-cylinder 115hp Waukesha engine and had a special low ratio Wisconsin double reduction rear axle.

The NEW STEWARTS
for 1934

The RESULT *of 22 years experience*

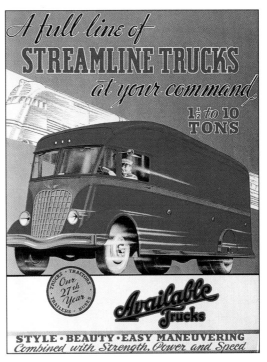

A full line of STREAMLINE TRUCKS *at your command*

1½ *to* 10 TONS

Our 27th Year TRUCKS · TRACTORS · TRAILERS · BUSES

Available Trucks

STYLE · BEAUTY · EASY MANEUVERING
Combined with Strength, Power and Speed

Although smaller makers had less money to spend, some managed to come up with extremely fascinating designs. Available, for example, introduced a full line of Streamline trucks in 1937. (left)

Stewart was a well respected name in the 1930s. Its heavy trucks did not come cheap — prices were comparable with Mack and White — but build quality was high. (right)

gasoline engines from Buda, Continental, LeRoi and Milwaukee. But the heyday of Stewart arrived in the early 1930s when heavy-duty truck models appeared powered by 6- and 8-cylinder Lycoming engines giving formidable outputs for the time of 100 and 130hp. Unlike most other manufacturers, Stewart offered its trucks with steel cabs and truck bodies ex-factory. In 1934 a line of new models with V-shaped radiator grille and a more contoured all-metal cab appeared. This new styling was initially only seen on lighter models, but later also reached the heavy-duty range. Six-wheelers with Truxmore attachment and sleepercab tractors became popular options for long-distance carriers. Stewarts were premium trucks, but did not come cheap. In 1932 the 7-ton Model 27XS

CONDOR
Diesel Oil Powered Motor Trucks

Economical — Attractive — Powerful

The Greatest Values in the Truck World
42 Different Models

Marmon-Herrington was the ancestor of small truck maker Marmon from Texas. Apart from converting Ford chassis, the company also made its own range of noteworthy 4x4 and 6x6 trucks.

Available made a good looking, honest product before the War. This attractive 2100 gallon streamlined milk tanker was built in cooperation with the Heil Co. in 1936.

with 6-cylinder engine, 12-speed transmission, Timken double reduction rear axle and Westinghouse air brakes was selling for the sum of $6190, on a par with the products of larger premium truck manufacturers, but Stewart claimed that its chassis would outlast nearly anything on the road by 5 to 10 years, and the company did indeed build up a very loyal following, notably overseas, exporting truck and bus chassis to nearly 40 different countries in the 1930s. However, production dwindled from 2315 units in 1930 to a meager 90 in 1939, resulting in bankruptcy only two years later.

A similar sad story was that of Republic a decade earlier. In the late 1910s the Republic Motor Truck Company of Michigan was a major force in the still young motor truck industry with annual sales of nearly 10,000 chassis. And just like Stewart, the conventionally assembled but sturdy Republic truck found many a willing buyer abroad, but in the end the company could not keep up with the times. In 1929 it merged with

The Condor truck was basically a Gramm export model and became best known outside the USA. It followed classic 1930s styling and was sold in over 30 countries until its demise in 1941.

American-LaFrance's truck division and for the next decade the products were labeled LaFrance-Republic. One of the most interesting designs to appear from this merger was a 20-ton six-wheeler in 1931. This 60mph beast was powered by a 240hp American-LaFrance V-12 gasoline engine, the same unit that was briefly offered in the Brockway Model V1200 three years later.

An equally impressive machine rolled off the assembly line of another small truck manufacturer, Relay Motors. In 1931 this maker's 'Duo-Drive' six-wheeler was launched

Only 12 of these Grass-Premier Superior Roadmaster GP tractors were produced in 1935/36. They were powered by a 85hp Ford V8 engine, but the last one built had a four-cylinder Cummins diesel.

with two Lycoming 8-cylinder engines mounted side-by-side under the hood. This arrangement delivered a healthy 275hp, enough for the Americans to claim it as 'the world's most powerful truck'. Relay was a combination of four different companies that also included Commerce, Garford and

Service truck makes. Relays were easily recognizable by their slanted louvers on the side of the hood and their steel spoke wheels. Technically, the trucks stood out for their pendulum drive rear axle arrangement that 'smothered horizontal impacts, improved traction, and greatly reduced tire and

In the 1930s, several Marmon-Herrington offroad desert buses were sold to the Middle-East. This huge 4x4 tractor was fitted with 4ft 2in high wheels and ran between Habbaniya and Damascus for the R.A.F. during World War II.

Before Available was taken over by CCC in 1957 it produced a distinguished range of heavy conventional and COE trucks. This C-Series double-drive six-wheeler dates from about 1942.

Between 1939 and 1953 a number of beautifully styled trucks appeared from the drawing board of J.L. Brown, chief engineer for Horton Motor Lines.

Although initially only built for the company's own use, the rugged Brown truck became available to other operators after the War. (also see below)

maintenance costs'. But innovative technical solutions and good looking designs could not prevent this famous small producer being forced into liquidation in 1932. During the Depression and thereafter, many more now-forgotten names would follow, including Condor, Gotfredson, LeMoon, Pierce-Arrow, Schacht, Selden and others, all of whom made some fine 'classic' trucks but were not able to achieve sufficiently high production runs to survive in the end.

There are very few small truck makers left in America. Marmon from Texas closed its doors in 1997, but started producing custom-built highway trucks in 1963 after some of the assets of the Marmon-Herrington company were acquired. These Model CHDT conventional and HDT cabover tractors with their characteristic designs date from those classic early years.

A classic from Mexico is the uniquely shaped Ramirez R22 Conventional, introduced around 1972. The strange bulges in the doors enable the driver to sleep on a makeshift couch across the cab.

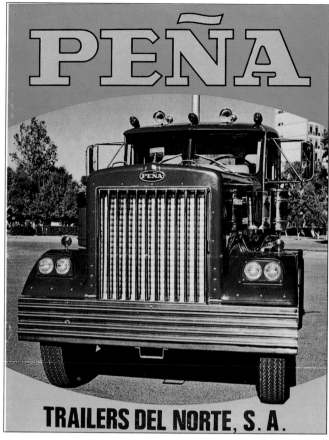

Relay was best known for the unusual pendulum rear axle set-up on its trucks, and in 1932 advertisements the company claimed its performance had saved truck owners millions of dollars.

The Mexican Peña closely resembled North American products of the time. The Cummins NTC-335 diesel powered 'Auto-Tractor' was built by Trailers del Norte S.A. of Monterrey in the late 1960s.

The last conventional built by Scot in Canada is undoubtly a 'classic to be'. This attractive Model A2HD tractor with bold fiberglass hood was introduced in 1976.

THE SPECIALISTS

Through the years virtually all the special truck makers have been smaller firms — keen specialists who were, and in some cases still are, willing and able to design and build any kind of truck the customer needs for a particular job. Engines, transmissions, axles and many other components are usually bought in from other manufacturers, as is done by the producers of custom built trucks. With production runs of as low as a few hundred chassis per year, coming up with a decent cab that met certain 'modern' requirements proved a difficult task for many specialists. Before the War it was found that even in off-highway trucks improved appearance could make a difference for the operator from an advertising standpoint. Problems arising from the costly design and

Judging from the radiator grille this early high wheeled dump truck could be a HUG. The truck was fitted with a hydraulic twin-ram hoist and body by the Heil Co.

Specialist truck makers have never tried to win any prizes in truck beauty contests, hence this early SuperTruck six-wheeler looks more utilitarian than attractive.

Although Corbitt became best known for its heavy-duty vehicles for the military, the North Carolina based company also built many good looking highway trucks in its 40 year history.

tooling of an up-to-date cab could be sometimes overcome by buying in a complete structure from one of the mass truck producers. As a consequence, quite a few special products, such as crane carriers, dump trucks, fire engines, utility vehicles, snow ploughs, wreckers, etc., appeared with a cab that was also standard on Diamond, Ford, or International truck chassis. Although specialist vehicles, just like normal trucks, are periodically restyled, this is mostly done from a desire to improve utility rather than looks, so improvements in appearance usually coincide with major technical changes.

Compared to highway trucks, special vehicles have often carried simpler bodywork because they are continuously subjected to rough handling. Off-highway trucks sported

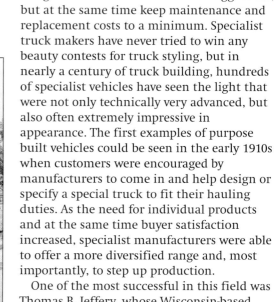

▶ Apart from building special custom units for many on/offroad uses, Ward-LaFrance also offered some excellent standardized models like this classic Model 25R from around 1934.

fenders and running boards that were designed so as to offer maximum ruggedness, but at the same time keep maintenance and replacement costs to a minimum. Specialist truck makers have never tried to win any beauty contests for truck styling, but in nearly a century of truck building, hundreds of specialist vehicles have seen the light that were not only technically very advanced, but also often extremely impressive in appearance. The first examples of purpose built vehicles could be seen in the early 1910s when customers were encouraged by manufacturers to come in and help design or specify a special truck to fit their hauling duties. As the need for individual products and at the same time buyer satisfaction increased, specialist manufacturers were able to offer a more diversified range and, most importantly, to step up production.

One of the most successful in this field was Thomas B. Jeffery, whose Wisconsin-based automobile company launched the famous Jeffery Quad 4x4 in 1913. It was a one ton 'seat-above-engine' truck and had a 36hp Buda 4-cylinder engine, 4-speed transmission, four wheel drive and four-wheel steering. In

In the 1930s Dart produced a complete line of 1.5 to 10 ton trucks and tractors. This sturdy 1930 dump truck for the County of Jackson looks well up to its task.

the first year over 5500 were produced, the majority for the US Army. From 1916 on it became known as the Nash Quad and it proved so successful that in 1918 the Army ordered 11,494 more units. This made Nash the world's largest truck manufacturer of the time. The tough off-road conditions of World War I had accelerated the development of four wheel drive trucks and by 1920 no less than 14 American manufacturers offered this type of vehicle.

Another company that was a true pioneer in the design of four wheel drive trucks was Duplex. This Michigan manufacturer came out in 1908 with a $^3/_4$-ton four wheel drive truck powered by a 20hp 'under-the-seat' 2-cylinder engine. In the early 1920s Duplex built a whole range of rather crude looking models with two and four wheel drive, and capacities up to 3.5 tons. Ten years later emphasis was placed on the production of more conventional trucks, such as the 3-ton Model SAC and by 1940 the range had extended to 10-ton truck and tractor models powered by 6-cylinder Buda or Hercules engines. The immediate postwar Duplex trucks were quite boxy designs that did not differ much in styling from the 1930s

Because of the seasonal nature of Oshkosh's sales to municipal and road-maintenance authorities, the company started to offer some on-highway models. This nicely styled F-model dates from 1932.

The handsome Corbitt Model 27BT Heavy Duty Tractor of 1934 was available with Corbitt's own gasoline or diesel powerplant, or with units from Hercules and Continental.

Ward LaFrance
MOTOR TRUCKS

MOTOR TRUCKS OF QUALITY

MODEL 156 SERIES

General Specifications:

Body Lengths	Tractor	10'	12'	14'	16'	18'
Cab to end of frame	104	120	144	168	192	216
Wheelbase	149½	157	172	187	200	214
Cab to center line of axle	71	78	93½	108½	122	135½
Length overall	223	239	262½	286½	310½	334½
Chassis weights—approximate	10000	10100	10200	10300	10400	10500
Cab weights	500	500	500	500	500	500
Axle ratio-standard	7.89-1	7.89-1	7.89-1	7.89-1	7.89-1	7.89-1
Governed speed	35	35	35	35	35	35
Tonnage—Gross Rating	32000	32000	32000	32000	32000	32000
Train Weight	50000	50000	50000	50000	50000	50000

Ward LaFrance
MOTOR TRUCKS

In 1936, Ward-LaFrance introduced this magnificently styled heavy-duty Model 156 conventional as an alternative to the medium-heavy 125-Series.

offerings, but they were impressive machines to look at, whether as a dump truck ploughing snow or as a highway tractor hauling a tanker. The 1950s saw the introduction of the much more streamlined L-Series two and four wheel drive trucks, Continental or Cummins powered, with Fuller transmission and Timken axle. It used the stylish 'Chicago' cab, as also fitted to several other 1950s trucks such as Cline, Diamond T, FWD, Hendrickson, International and Oshkosh. The latter became one of the trendsetters in the manufacturing of specialist vehicles. Oshkosh's first four wheel drive truck appeared in 1917, incorporating such novelties as pneumatic tires, a locking center differential, and roller bearings on the

The Oshkosh Model J 2-tonner was new on the market in 1935 and was a very pleasing design with its streamlined fenders and V-type radiator grille.

This 1935 Corbitt is a rare sight. This sumptuous model was exported to Europe and used the fenders and some other body panels from the famous Auburn car.

steering pivots of the front axle. In the early 1920s the 4x4 range was based on the 6-cylinder Model H, which offered a payload up to five tons. Unlike some other specialists who supplied huge numbers of vehicles to the US Army, Oshkosh sold most of its four wheel drive trucks to civilian operators. One reason was that the military mainly needed vehicles with a capacity of 1,5 tons, while the Wisconsin company produced much heavier units. The US Army argued that they could not afford the price that Oshkosh asked for these premium heavy-duty trucks. Nevertheless, with road building and construction across America at a peak, Oshkosh did very well in the 1920s and '30s, selling hundreds of tough special purpose vehicles to construction companies, road maintenance authorities, civil engineering contractors, and other private, municipal, and federal bodies. In 1932 a massive 44,000 pound GVW model powered by a 200hp engine with a 12-speed transmission was introduced, proving an ideal machine for the attachment of a giant V-shaped snow plow. It was just what the road crews needed to keep the mountain passes open in the long winters of some parts of the East and the Northwest.

In the 1930s, hauliers became more and more aware of the need to use specialized equipment for certain applications, which led the industry to develop better vocational trucks. Clearly, a dump truck or fire engine required a different technical approach than a rig hauling a load of toys or beer. Hence Oshkosh found itself building larger and more powerful special application vehicles, such as the 10-ton Model GD 4x4 with 6-

cylinder Hercules HXD engine, and later Cummins diesel as well. Although the shape of this truck was conservative, it certainly looked impressive with its square hood and sturdy steel cab sitting high on the chassis. In 1935 a more streamlined model appeared as the J-Series. It had a slanted radiator grille and long contoured fenders, and the old-fashioned sun visor above the windshield had disappeared. This handsome styling probably helped it to sell even in some highway applications. The J-Series cab spread to other Oshkosh models too, together with a more gently rounded radiator grille. After the war, a distinctive feature became the unusually long nose seen on some Oshkosh models. To meet the needs of the growing ready mix concrete market, an all wheel-drive chassis with excellent maneuverability

Walter introduced its first four wheel drive truck in 1911 and has concentrated ever since on the manufacture of vehicles for specialized needs. This big 8-axle train was developed for a Canadian client in 1936 to haul heavy reels of paper.

▼ Hendrickson truck design, be it conventional or COE, had many faces during the 1930s and '40s. Some models had intriguing front end styling, like this 1939 example.

In the mid-1930s FWD developed a range of attractive truck and tractor models, with pontoon-type fenders and a long high hood, for commercial transportation duties.

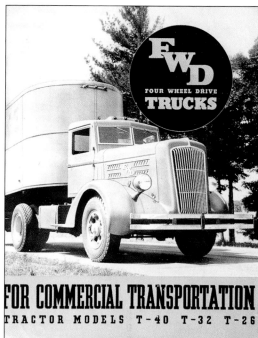

FOR COMMERCIAL TRANSPORTATION
TRACTOR MODELS T-40 T-32 T-26

A scene from a Chicago backstreet in 1948. This Hendrickson heavy-duty diesel tractor can be recognized by its radiator grille, which later also adorned the 1950s models with more streamlined cabs.

▼ This big, potent 6x6 ex-forces Biederman C2 or F1-model found a new application in 1946 on heavy hauling duties for a Pennsylvanian operator.

and weight distribution was designed. This was achieved by moving the engine as far forward as possible and setting the front driving axle way back. It looked peculiar, but it worked well and the idea was later adopted by other specialist manufacturers, including FWD.

The 'Four Wheel Drive' truck, or FWD for short, was born in a machine shop in Clintonville, Wisconsin, back in 1912. First to appear were light FWD commercials based on passenger cars, but World War I requirements urged the company to design a range of 3- and 5-ton capacity all wheel drive military type trucks. In the end over 15,000 Model B cab-over-engine trucks saw service in the US

Army. They proved indispensable on the battlefields of Europe and after the war FWDs, and also American Peerless four wheel drive trucks, were even assembled in Great Britain for a while. Although FWD concentrated between the Wars on special purpose vehicles for such diverse vocations as snow-plowing, fire-fighting, road construction and maintenance, logging, mining, and oilfield duties, some beautifully styled highway models also appeared when FWD offered a range of heavy conventionals known as the T-Series in 1936. The medium-heavy T-26 and T-32 tractors could be recognized by a V-type radiator grille and a one-piece slanted windscreen, while the heavy T-40 and T-60 conventionals had pontoon style fenders, bullet type headlights and a V-shaped windscreen. Pulling a semi-trailer and nicely liveried these big FWDs made a fine sight on the highway, causing one Wisconsin operator to remark of his new coal hauling T-40 that 'its advertising value has been set at $5000'.

A cab-over-engine version of the T-32 was launched in 1937, a rather lofty machine with a wide slanted radiator grille. When noted industrial designer Brooks Stevens restyled the T-Series conventionals in 1939, giving them a more rounded hood and cab line, the high COE also received a streamlining job. The style change in cabovers would last well into the 1940s with several combined

After the war Dart resumed the production of highway trucks such as this custom-built long-nosed conventional fitted with a cab made by Diamond-T.

FWD/Brooks Stevens prototypes appearing. Some of the Stevens styling efforts were really beautiful, but in the end they proved much too expensive for FWDs limited highway truck market to produce. Before the War, engines fitted in highway chassis were mainly Waukesha, FWD's own 6-cylinder 85-, 110- and 125hp units, or, from 1938 onwards, more powerful Cummins diesels.

When World War II broke out the Americans were fortunate that the truck industry could already look back on two decades of experience in the manufacturing of all wheel drive trucks. As a result the time needed between the Army order, the design of the trucks, and the actual delivery of quantities of specialized vehicles was a lot shorter than the development of some other war products. Most truck components specified by the US Armed Forces, such as front driving wheels, tandem drive rear axles, auxiliary transmissions, transfer boxes, heavy-duty suspension systems, etc., had at one time or another been developed for the civilian industry, albeit on a very limited scale, and it was only when the war had ended that the use of tandem-drive and 6x6 trucks became more common among civilian operators. Despite its tremendous experience in the manufacture of conventional 6x6 vehicles, the bulk of FWD's war time involvement centered around the production of civilian-styled Model CU and SU cabover tractors and trucks. In the 1950s FWD introduced a new series of conventionals fitted with the popular 'Chicago' cab, as also

▼ In contrast with other ex-World War II trucks, the heavy FWD SU COE was less popular among civilian operators, but this rugged looking truck and trailer was used by the Netherlands Railways to transport Marshall Aid goods from ports to various European inland destinations.

▶ Around 1951 a Corbitt COE with an unusually high cab appeared on the market. With an eye level almost 10 feet above the road the cab was meant to give the driver an unparalleled view all around.

used extensively by International. Another shared cab adorned the FWD COE of 1958 in the form of the familiar C-Series Ford cab, which could also be seen on the N-Series Mack and on Hendrickson offerings.

Hendrickson is a name not to be missed when it comes to noting the many classic on- and off-highway trucks that American firms have brought us over the years. This company, originating in Chicago, was well known for its broad range of high quality, special purpose vehicles for over 75 years. We must also not forget the famous Hendrickson tandem axle suspension system, which was first an International truck exclusive and from 1948 widely used by other manufacturers. Hendrickson was a pioneer in the production of cab-over-engine chassis. In fact its first models, which appeared between 1910 and 1913, were of this design. The company was also one of the first to come up with an enclosed cab that could be tilted to 90 degrees for easy access. In 1932 a new generation of large capacity but compactly built cabover models was introduced. It put Hendrickson in the forefront of COE design, but in the early 1930s the preference was for conventional trucks, and the advanced

cabover did not attract as much business as the company had hoped. Hendrickson did not sit still, however, and developed a new range of custom-built four- and six-wheeled conventional trucks. It included 6x4 models fitted with Hendrickson's own unique equalizing beam suspension. By 1936 there was a choice of payload from 2.5 to 12 tons. Engines fitted were mainly Waukesha, with

A magnificent classic: a fully decked out Ward-LaFrance D-Series conventional from 1950. This sturdy model sported an angular hood and military style fenders.

Cummins as an option from 1938, and Caterpillar available a bit later still. Hendrickson styling, be it conventional or cabover, varied widely during the 1930s and '40s. Some trucks were angular, no-frills designs, others had beautifully contoured hood and fender lines with a uniquely executed radiator grille. In 1940 the characteristic hood and radiator grille disappeared again when Hendrickson decided to fit a more simplified front end and use the standard International KB-cab for its new conventional A-Series trucks. In 1950 a similar connection came about when the all-new Hendrickson B-Series conventional and COE trucks appeared with the familiar IHC 'Comfo-Vision' cab. In later years also some Hendrickson COEs came equipped with the International CO-405 sleepercab and the Diamond-T tilt cab — all this in addition to several, sometimes short-lived, cab-forward designs of their own. Despite production that seldom exceeded 100 (custom-built) chassis per year, Hendrickson was clearly not afraid to experiment with truck styling!

In 1953 Cline started to build 'badge-engineered' Hendrickson conventional trucks for the construction industry. Initially, production was very low at a few dozen chassis per year. But when heavier models for mining, logging and oilfield duties, and special crane carriers and railroad trucks were developed in the 1960s, Cline's sales

climbed to a more healthy level. Like Cline, other specialists, such as CCC, Coleman and Canadian Sicard, offered a custom built on/off-highway truck in the 1950s and '60s equipped with IHC's 'Comfo-Vision' cab. Thus, this well thought out and sturdy cab with its sleek lines became a real classic in its own right.

Since the early 1920s the list of special application truck and trailer makers has been long and varied. More famous names springing to mind in this respect are Biederman, Corbitt, Dart, Ward-LaFrance and Walter. The latter became best known for its all wheel drive 'Snow Fighter', with 'four-

Military influence was also evident in this c.1948 Duplex Model J-HA tractor. Hooked up to a Fruehauf tanker it made a good looking rig, but Duplex became better known for its specialist vehicles.

A typical feature of the Oshkosh Model 1834 was the protuding snout. By moving the engine as far forward as possible and the front axle back, better weight distribution was achieved.

With its sloping wire mesh radiator grille and slanted front windshield, the Corbitt Model H25 was an easily recognizable heavy truck in 1949.

point positive drive' system, that was introduced around 1937. Walters were easily identified by their long, round snouts and front axle set well back. This arrangement not only helped achieve a better weight distribution, but also offered much improved engine accessibility. And it sure looked 'macho'!

Dart entered the ultra heavy-duty field in the late 1930s, having for over 30 years built mostly chassis for highway operation. In 1938 the range consisted of medium to heavy conventionals for weights up to 10 tons in six-

wheeler form. In addition to special trucks for the mining and logging industry, production of highway trucks was resumed after the War with a handsome line of conventionals for GVWs up to 20 tons, but with competition at a peak, few were built, and from mid-1950 onwards Dart decided to concentrate fully on the design and production of custom-built off-highway dump trucks.

Biederman, Corbitt, and Ward-LaFrance became best known for their contribution to the 1940-45 war effort. 6x6 drive military cargo trucks and wreckers were turned out by the thousands and wartime profits enabled these specialists to take up civilian production again in a big way. Where Biederman's vast range of highway trucks from pre-war days did not differ much in design and appearance from other contemporary offerings, the 1947 Model NS

Before Dart concentrated solely on the production of heavy-duty trucks for the mining industry, it designed some good looking highway models such as this slippery COE from 1935.

Four new Coleman trucks ready for delivery outside the factory in Littleton, Colorado. These 4x4 type units date from about 1945/46 and the cabs were sourced from either Ford or GM.

conventional looked much more the part with its sloping hood and chrome trimmed radiator grille. Ward-LaFrance hailed from New York state, and its best years were probably the late 1940s when a new conventional model, the D-Series, sporting an angular cab and military styled hood and fenders was introduced. Heaviest in the range was the D-5, with Cummins HB-600 diesel engine and a Fuller 5A-920 5-speed transmission. Total Ward-LaFrance truck production for 1947 amounted to 509, while

a year later it was down to 271 units. Last but not least we must mention Corbitt, a legendary US Army and Allied Forces supplier during World War II. The wartime success of the big 6x6 drive Model 50 SD6 cargo carrier/ heavy haulage tractor helped Corbitt achieve good sales with new highway models on the civilian market in the late 1940s and the 1950s. Based in Henderson, North Carolina, the company offered a well-designed line of conventionals in 1948. These long-nosed models sported a sharply raked

Yet another rare Corbitt is this snub-nosed conventional with integral sleeper from 1954. Corbitts shared some sheet metal with the Brown designs of the same era.

The Walter Tractor-Truck of 1947 with its imposing round nose and unique 'Four Point Positive Drive' can truly be labeled a classic in the specialist vehicle league.

Cline trucks were custom built to fit specific haulage jobs. This 4x2 model resembled a Hendrickson conventional and was equipped with the famous International 'Comfo-Vision' cab.

radiator grille and had a wide cab with slanted one or two piece windshield. 1952 saw a new model with a more rounded, upright radiator grille. This, the last conventional to appear before Corbitt's unfortunate demise in 1958, was available with a 6-cylinder Continental gasoline engine or a diesel unit from Hercules or Cummins. From a distance, the handsomely styled Corbitt looked a bit like the equally impressive 1950s Brown conventional. Today, both are fondly remembered examples of classic heavy-duty trucks made with pride and craftsmanship by small and specialist truck manufacturers who, for whatever reason, could not keep up with the times.

The same International cab was also fitted to this handsome FWD Model T6-405. Although most FWDs were used in specialist operations, this rugged unit proved a good highway tractor for Steffke Freight Co. of Warsaw, Illinois, in 1957.

This big and bold owner-driven Hendrickson BD-
Series tractor with integral sleeper and lots of extra
goodies made for an impressive sight in 1963.

Sicard of Canada became famous for its specialist products for the construction industry and snow-clearing. From 1958 on it also offered some good looking highway models.

The first Ibex appeared in 1964. They were made in Salt Lake City, Utah, and came in 4x4, 6x4 and 6x6 drive configurations with an aluminum cab and a narrow or wide fiberglass hood.

Cook Bros offered a range of Reo-based construction trucks under the name of 'Load King' from 1956. They were equipped with what they called a 'Profit-Placed' cab design that permitted a greater payload.

FWD Tractioneers were mostly used as rigid dumps and concrete mixers, but this awesome 4x4 drive unit pulled a semitrailer. Note the set forward fifth wheel and the Dodge cab fitted.

A colorful ad of the late 1960s FWD Forward Mover Model CO5 with its peculiar forward-slanting windshield. This was the short-lived predecessor of the more shapely CO64-Series COE.

To capture a greater share of the highway market in, 1963 Hendrickson introduced the snub-nosed Model BD-270. These short 94 inch BBC tractors rode on Hendrickson Tandem suspensions.

Although construction trucks are also restyled periodically, this is done more from a desire to improve utility than looks. Even so, the sight of this stained but honest Hendrickson BD-640 Tri-Axle rear dump at work on the Indiana Toll Road in June 1970 is a real treat.

Photo Index